HEAVEN

Books by Al Young

Dancing (poems)

Snakes (novel)

The Song Turning Back into Itself (poems)

Who Is Angelina? (novel)

Geography of the Near Past (poems)

Sitting Pretty (novel)

Ask Me Now (novel)

Bodies & Soul (musical memoirs)

The Blues Don't Change: New and Selected Poems

Kinds of Blue (musical memoirs)

Things Ain't What They Used to Be (musical memoirs)

Seduction by Light (novel)

Mingus/Mingus: Two Memiors (with Janet Coleman)

Heaven: Collected Poems 1956–1990

HEAVEN
Collected Poems 1956–1990

Al Young

Creative Arts Book Company
Berkeley
1992

The author gratefully acknowledges the editors of the following publications in whose pages many of these poems, some in slightly different form, first appeared:

Aftermath of Invisibility (Xavier University), *Aldebaran Review, Alpha Sort, American Rag, Beloit Poetry Journal, Black Dialogue, Black on Black, Black Mountain Press, Black Scholar, Brilliant Corners, California Poets Anthology* (Second Coming Press), *Callaloo, Camels Coming, Chelsea, Chicago Review, Confrontation, Counter/Measures, Crystalline Flight, Decal* (Cardiff Wales), *Dices* (Houghton Mifflin Co.), *Egg, El Corno Emplumado* (Mexico City), *Epoch* (Cornell University), *Essence, Evergreen, Foothill Quarterly* (Foothill Community College), *Galley Sail Review, Guabi, Hambone, Hanging Loose, Hubbub, Illuminations, Iowa Review, Jeopardy* (Western Washington University), *Journal for the Protection of All Beings* (City Lights Books), *Journal of Black Poetry, Konch, The Lit, Love (Incorporating Hate), Loveletter, Loves, Etc.* (Doubleday/Anchor), *Massachusetts Review, Mosaic: Literature & Ideas* (University of Manitoba Press), *Mother Jones, mule teeth, Natural Process* (Hill & Wang), *The New Black Poetry* (International Publishers), *New Directions, New Orleans Review* (Loyola University), *New York Review of Books* (Antaeus Selection), *Nexus, Ploughshares, Obsidian, 100 Flowers, Paris Review, Perspectives, Place, Quarry* (University of California at Santa Cruz), *Quilt, River Styx, Rogue River Gorge, San Francisco Bay Guardian, San Miguel Review* (Mexico), *Sequoia* (Stanford University), *Solid Ground, Sponge, Think* (IBM), *Threepenny Review, TriQuarterly, 23 California Poets, Umoja, Umbra, Willow Springs* (Eastern Washington State University), *WPA, Wine & Oil Anthology* (Bombay), *Works, Yardbird Reader,* and *Y'Bird.*

Miller Williams translated the lines by Chilean poet Nicanor Parra quoted in the long poem, "Dancing."

The passage from *The Pillow Book of Sei Shōnagon* was translated by Arthur Waley.

The poem by Li Chin-fa that introduces "The Song Turning Back into Itself" was translated by Kai-yu Hsu.

Walter Albert translated the line by Blaise Cendrars that precedes "Maya."

ISBN: 0-88739-068-4 Cloth
      0-88739-069-2 Paper

Library of Congress Catalogue Card Number: 92-73681

Design: Charles Fuhrman Design
Original cover art by Stephen Henriques

For information Contact: Creative Arts Book Co.
833 Bancroft Way • Berkeley, California 94710

Printed in the United States of America

The future enters into us,
in order to transform itself in us,
long before it happens.

Rainer Maria Rilke

All the way to heaven is heaven.

Saint Teresa

Author's Note

The placement of poems in this volume has been kept as straightforward as possible. Four previous books — *Dancing* (1969), *The Song Turning Back into Itself* (1971), *Geography of the Near Past* (1976), and *The Blues Don't Change: New and Selected Poems*, 1982 — are presented in their original order, spelling and punctuation. These are followed by chronological groupings of published and unpublished poetry composed between 1956 and 1990, but uncollected until now. Included are three entirely new collections: *By Heart* (1982–85), *22 Moon Poems* (1984–85), and *See Level* (1986–90).

— A. Y.

Table of Contents

SEVEN STEPS TO *HEAVEN:*
An Introduction to Al Young and His Poetry

O.O. Gabugah

Long as I been knowing my man Al Young, it still shocked me when Donald S. Ellis, his publisher, just flat out suggested I write the introduction to this whopping collection of Al's poetry, which runs all the way back to the Fifties. I'll tell you straight off the top that this really flattered me because, for one thing, it meant that somebody thought enough of me and my abilities and opinions to think I could handle the job. For another, it meant I'd finally get a chance to tell the world about the brother who helped put me on the map back in the early Seventies when — coming like I was from the aural tradition — I was too shy and self-conscious to write my own poems down.

Personally speaking, me and Al Young only go back together as far as the early Sixties, when he was still running around with a guitar and an armload of books, records and notebooks. That was where I walked in the door; that's the Al Young that first attracted my attention. That would nail the time down to 1960. The place: New York City. It was summertime, I remember, and my man had blown into town from Ann Arbor, Michigan with some other college guys, and all of 'em played music. Bob Detwiler played tenor sax, Bruce Wigel played bass, Ron Rogers was an alto sax man; Perry Lederman and Marc Silber were guitar players and Al himself picked a little guitar too, but mostly he could sing — and I mean the boy could sing! And he knew a whole lot about jazz too, and was doing some hanging out with that strange, crazy dude named Mingus. He and Perry and Marc, they were into this folk music stuff, which I always thought was on the corny side, but they kept themselves a gig.

When I first caught Al he was sitting up on a stool in some little joint on Bleecker Street, directly across from the Gaslight Café, and he was running through these blues and Mexican tunes and oldtimey stuff from all downsouth. You wanna know the truth, I felt a little ashamed of what he was doing because, well, some of them old slavery songs and ignorant country music was stuff I thought black people needed to cut loose. Back then I was into Sam Cooke and Dinah Washington and Les McCann and Horace Silver and Cannonball Adderley and Bobby Timmons. You know, for a 15-year-old, hey, I was pretty hip.

So what was I doing down there in the Village? We all used to go down there Friday night to see what we could get into. It's kind of a funny thing to look back on, but that was how it was then. The white boys'd be busy tryna bust uptown to Harlem to get next to the sisters and all that good weed we had up there, and we'd be busting our ass to get down to the Village and talk us up on some of them pretty little kosher kiddies and Italian stallions. Crazy, ain't it?

So I'd walked in this joint to get off the crowded street and it wasn't any problem because it was a coffeehouse; nobody was sweating me being underage. And there was Al Young, singing away and strumming on his guitar. And the women, oooweee! I swear, they were all crowding in around him like mosquitoes! So I thought to myself: Listen, Franklin Delano Watson — which is what I was known as in them days — either you're gonna have to learn to play guitar and sing or else you're gonna have to get to know this Al Young a little bit better.

When the set was over, I went up and introduced myself. We talked about first one thing and another, then he told me what he really was tryna do was write. My eyes lit up then. "Look," I told him, "that's what I wanna get into eventually. You know, like poetry. I been reading Langston Hughes and tryna do song lyrics, and I believe I got a little talent for poetry."

Al smiled and said, "Well, the main thing is you gotta keep writing. It doesn't even matter what." He reached into his guitar case and took out a thick buncha pages that looked half-typed and half-handwritten.

"What's this?" I asked.

"It's a letter I've been writing to a friend, an old school-mate back in Detroit named Mary Lewis."

"A letter?" I said. "But it's more than fifty pages long."

"That's right," said Al. "It's a letter that's also a journal and a travelogue and a novella and a prose-poem all rolled up in one. Everytime I get a chance, I'll sit down and add a little something to it, just for the fun of it, just to see how what's in my heart and on my mind and is gonna come out looking on paper."

That's how we met. It was only a few weeks before Al would move out to the West Coast and start up a new life for himself. Or maybe he was only just starting his life for real.

▼　▼　▼

A lot of what I've since learned about the pre-1960 Al Young I've picked up from being around him and his friends and, quite naturally, from reading his fiction and essays and articles.

But it's the poetry I keep coming back to, and not just because that's what interests me most. What I like about the man's poems is that they're coming out of the same tradition I'm coming out of, which is a tradition where people be talking with one another. Now, a lot's been said about Call-and-Response and the Amen Corner and all these dynamics that seem to go with the way black people communicate, which is to say the way African and Afro-whatever people communicate. But all you gotta do to understand how there's two sides to this communication thing is to read Al Young. Al Young talks to the reader. In fact, he himself is all the time going around saying, "No piece of writing is complete until it's been read and the reader hears what's being said and answers. In a sense, readers are the co-writers of whatever they happen to be reading."

I'm with Al on that point: A musician without dancers or listeners, a preacher without a congregation, a writer with nobody out there to hear or see or taste or smell or feel the stuff you're writing about — well, that's something like tryna make love all by yourself, ain't it? Don't get me wrong. It *can* be done; I do know that. But it isn't much fun, is it?

Most poetry — especially of the modern, right-now persuasion — isn't much fun, either. Not to my way of listening and talking. When I read mosta what people are writing and pushing nowadays, I get the idea that the poets quite often are saying something like: "Kiss my ass, chump! I'm a poet, that's

[3]

what! Besides, if you were even vaguely capable of getting at what's going on in my vast and brilliant mind, you wouldn't be sitting here at this poetry reading or holed up in the library checking me out; you'd be out there or up here doing your own thing, blowing other people's minds!"

Don't you get the idea that this is what all these high-strung, hard-to-understand poets are saying? First of all, most poetry today is about somebody's pitiful little hurt feelings (they don't take too many chances with big feelings anymore), or else it's a joke of some kind, which I think the stand-up comics at the comedy clubs can do better. Or else it's some kinda poems whose whole point is to let you know how bad and well-read the poet that wrote it is. They be writing poems *about* poems about *poems*, and be quoting lines and passages that's so obscure you'd have to be a Ph.D or some type of scholar to really understand what it is that's being referred to.

Since I don't have time for these silly-ass games — plus I don't read or write poetry, in the first place, to prove how deep and heavy and intellectual I am — just give me somebody that's hitting on the main subject, which is life. And it's a double treat when that somebody also happens to be full of life while they're talking about life. That's Al Young. And the brother is upbeat; about as upbeat as you can get and still be living in North America in, you might as well say, the 21st Century. That's what I read poetry for: I wanna know what you love, what you're crazy about; whether it's a certain hangup or fixation or just being alive or wanting your freedom from something that's been holding you down. What I've noticed about too many well-meaning professional poets is that they're See No Evil, Hear No Evil, and Evil.

The poetry scene itself, as a matter of fact, is something Al has never really felt comfortable in. Like the literary scene in general, which he finds to be trifling, shallow and mean-spirited, the poetry scene, the way Al's experienced it, either tends to be doofus or dull. He talks about this a little in his novel *Sitting Pretty*; that chapter where Sidney J. Prettymon and his pal Willie G. drop in on this poetry night event at JoJo's Let's Get It On Club in San Francisco and, lo and behold, who should they catch doing his hot poetry act — and

[4]

knocking the crowd on its collective butt — but Yours Truly.

The scene is pretty mean, tho; I can testify to that my own-self. Sometimes it's like there's too many pigs and not enough slops, so what you get is all this oinking and grunting and push-ing and shoving and squabbling at the trough. I don't mean to muddy poetry, which I love as much as Al does, but I do mean to demean the greedy, stuffy personalities of an awful lotta — well, let's just call 'em poetry types.

Far as I can tell, Al Young is not a poetry type and, even back in public school, when he was writing all them bad books (and I'm talking about bad for real) with titles like *Still Life and Blue Wine*, or *City Morning Pattern*, or *Dragon's Teeth*, or *Fresh Thunder*, he didn't take himself too seriously. I ain't saying he wasn't intense, but he knew better than to jump up and go to getting too serious about it.

He's a poet whose roots run all the way back to Mississippi and front-porch storytelling, and to listening at everything — crickets, the wind and how it plays the trees, the sound water makes, rain, cows, chickens, dogs, mosquitoes, mules going hee-haw, people laughing or tryna talk when they're all choked up over something. You need to know that, even today, Al is still the great listener and hearer. When he was little, his grand-mother used to tease him about parking himself in a corner of the kitchen, tuning in Arthur Godfrey and sipping on a cup of hot tea. And his father was one of them amateur radio opera-tors; I think they called 'em hams. Al loved to sit up and put his ear to the receiver and dial in all the overseas stations and shortwave bands he could get, like he was some kinda global safecracker or something. That's still him! The other day I helped him hook up a fancy new TV set he'd just bought. The minute we got the thing wired up right and made sure the an-tenna and the video recorder were working, Al sighed and fell back in a big old chair and snapped on one of his favorite radios so he could listen at this program about blues singer Big Joe Turner they were doing on National Public Radio.

You gotta remember that Al's been a disk jockey, going all the way back to his teens in Detroit. He's told me about those days, before he even got to work on a real station, when he and his buddy Leon Reynolds would sit up in their rooms and spin records and talk just like they were broadcasting. Platters and chatter is what they were still calling it in the Fifties. They'd even look up businesses in the phone book and write their own commercials to read "over the air."

And I don't have to tell you how much time my man spent listening at all those old classic radio shows in the Forties and Fifties: "Dimension X," the original "Gunsmoke," "The Fat Man," "Lux Presents Hollywood," "Radio Mystery Theater," and such. Plus, and this is important to know, Al lived right there across the river from Windsor, Ontario, which gave him the opportunity to pick up all that good-sounding, different-sounding radio from the Canadian Broadcasting Company. They'd be running this thing called "Jazz Unlimited" on Saturdays with Dick MacDougal, and they'd have high-tone plays and dramas, documentaries about salmon fishing and what was happening with the Eskimos, and there'd be live symphony and pop music, and shows from England and New Zealand, and stuff in French. But the important thing to remember is this: Aside from all that great variety of programs, the CBC was a place where you could actually hear people reading their poetry over the radio. And it was after he got used to hearing people read their jive in their own voices and out of their own selves that Al understood what poets were doing.

Now don't get me wrong. Al was always a greedy reader. From the time he was three, he'd been tearing thru books and libraries. From what he's told me, he musta gobbled up everything they'd let him check outta the poetry and literature parta the Detroit Public Library over there on Woodward Avenue near the Detroit Institute of Arts. When you're going thru this collection, *Heaven*, you're not gonna run up on a strange little thing Al dreamed up while he was still at Central High School back in the mid-Fifties. But I wish he'd included it. *L'Enfant de Fer* is what he called it: *Iron Child*. He showed it to me one night while I was visiting and he was going thru some old boxes and showing me how strange he thought his early stuff was.

"What's this?" I asked, reaching for this *Iron Child* thing.

"Oh," he said, "this dates all the way back to my Rimbaud period."

"Your *what* period?"

"Rimbaud," Al said again.

I'da swore he was saying Rambo, you know, like Sylvester Stallone. But he explained about this dude Jean Arthur Rimbaud over there in France in the 1800s, and how he'd written up all this amazing shit before he was 19 and then said "Fuck it!" and hobo'd his way to Africa, where he started running slaves and guns.

"Damn!" I told Al. "It's always the crazy ones that get into the poetry business, ain't it?

Al laughed and said, "If you've got the nerve to call it a business."

Since I never was a bona fide fool, I went to the library after Mr. Ellis said he wanted me to introduce this book of Al's, and I did me some boning up on the brother. I mean, I think I know the meat and blood of what the brother's all about; it's the bones of it that needed polishing. I was flabbergasted at how much'd already been written about him and his work. But there was a statement Al made years ago himself, about where he was coming from, that I think is worth quoting.

In *Contemporary Poets*, put out by St. Martin's Press, Al Young says his poetry is "characterized by a marked personal and lyrical mysticism as well as a concern with social and spiritual problems of contemporary man in a technological environment that grows hourly more impersonal and unreal. My favorite themes are those of love, the infinite changeability of the world as well as its eternal changelessness, and the kind of meaning (both private and universal) that flowers out of everyday life. My influences in general have been Black culture and popular speech (Southern rural and urban U.S.) and music in particular."

Al goes on to put his finger on some of those influences: "Afro-American folk and popular music, Caribbean music of both English- and Spanish-speaking peoples); American Indian poetry and song; Hindu philosophy." And when it comes to talking about poets he admired and maybe learned a little something from, the list of names he dropped includes the poetry of the Bible, Li Po, Rabinadrath Tagore, Vladimir Mayakovsky, Federico García Lorca, early T.S. Eliot, Leopold Senghor, Nicolás Guillén, Blaise Cendrars, Kenneth Rexroth, LeRoi

Jones, Nicanor Parra and Denise Levertov. From knowing him, however, I could add plenty other names to that list, even tho I know how much Al hates putting lists like this together. The worst thing you can ask him is who his favorite poets are. He probably wouldn't mind if I just squeezed in Omar Khayyam, Miguel de Cervantes Saavedra, Samuel Taylor Coleridge, John Keats, Percy Bysshe Shelley, Emily Dickinson, Walt Whitman, Paul Laurence Dunbar, Edgar Lee Masters, Langston Hughes, Dylan Thomas, Gabriela Mistral, e.e. cummings, Kenneth Patchen, Gwendolyn Brooks, Julia Fields, Bob Kaufman and Victor Hernández Cruz.

"There is no end to the making of lists," Al Young once wrote me in a postcard from Yugoslavia. Which brings me to another thing: My man gets around, and I don't mean just physically. From the minute I first got to know him back there in New York, Al never wasted a minute when it came to getting someplace. With only a few dollars in his pocket he didn't think anything of hopping on a bus and traveling deep down into Mexico, or sailing overseas someplace or, for that matter, I get dizzy just looking at how he's been running up and down *this* country, these New Knighted States, for all these decades. For me, he moves in and outta territories of the mind and spirit the same way he zips around this sweet old planet Earth.

You could read most American poetry they put out now and never know the world order was changing. As far as that kinda thing goes, you couldn't hardly tell from reading mosta what poets put out that people were starving and hurting and fighting back all over the globe, that the Yankee dollar isn't the flag-waving measure of everything like it used to be, that the so-called Third World ain't necessarily coming in third no more.

Al Young and I do and probably always will have our little differences — which are mainly political — but what keeps making me go soft on his stuff is the same thing that yanked me into poetry in the first place: It'll make you feel good about being alive. I happen to believe that feeling good about yourself is better than all the smack, crack, coke, smoke and booze in the world; it's even more important than being rich and famous and powerful. But, see, there I go jamming my personal opinions all up in your face again.

All this money they're spending tryna bust up the dope traffic and educate and rehabilitate people about drugs — it's all a waste until you realize what Al meant in that poem of his called "For Poets," with the last line that goes: "Don't forget to fly." It comes down to being a spirit problem, don't you think? Not being connected with anything; not even your ownself.

So now we come to the seven steps, which are all built up from my favorite Al Young sayings. It's interesting to flip thru these "spindrift pages," as Dylan Thomas liked to call 'em, and get an idea about how the poet finally started getting his voice (and voices) together down across the seasons. It's occurred to me you might find it pleasurable to keep these particular lines and licks in mind while you're reading around in this very special book from my pal Al, who, by the way, actually believes what they express.

(1) All beginnings start right here
(2) Nothing ever happened that wasn't dreamed
(3) Where are you before you even get born?
(4) The moon is your face/in the window of the world
(5) The sun is shining in my backdoor/right now
(6) Eye to eye/with yourself at last
(7) We move already thru a low-pitched heaven

— O.O. Gabugah
Harlem, New York

Dancing
(1969)

Do you love me /
now that I can dance?

The Contours

A DANCE FOR MILITANT DILETTANTES

No one's going to read
or take you seriously,
a hip friend advises,
until you start coming down on them
like the black poet you truly are
& ink in lots of black in your poems
soul is not enough
you need real color
shining out of real skin
nappy snaggly afro hair
baby grow up & dig on *that!*

You got to learn to put in about
stone black fists
coming up against white jaws
& red blood splashing
down those fabled wine & urine-
stained hallways
black bombs blasting out real white estate
the sky itself black with what's to come:
final holocaust
the settling up

Dont nobody want no nice nigger no more
these honkies man that put out
these books & things
they want an angry splib
a furious nigrah
they dont want no bourgeois woogie
they want them a militant nigger
in a fiji haircut
fresh out of some secret boot camp
with a bad book in one hand
& a molotov cocktail in the other
subject to turn up at one of their conferences
or soirées
& shake the shit out of them

DANCING DAY TO DAY

In my street
the people mostly go.
Very few come
to what I'd call home.

We earn our wages
cash our checks
park our cars
manage our packages
receive our mail
whistle our tunes
sweep our porches
& draw our curtains
in public.

My neighbors are
black
mexican
japanese
chinese
even a young couple from India
& straight-out ordinary gringos
(one of whom
strolls her senile bull terrier
around the block
twilights
with a baseball bat).

They dont go climbing
the lemontree
or shaking the appletree
out back for fun.
They mow their lawns
smoke their grass
crank up the stereo
or the TV volume
evenings

or wash dolls
& set them out to dry.

One of my favorites
is the little boy
whose new bike gets a flat
or who mopes across the schoolyard
kicking stones
like little footballs.

Best of all
since moving here
I like going for walks
or for drowsy car rides
with the glamorous woman
in the stylish clothes
who loves newspapers
magazines
& lives in number 2.

When she knocks at my door
frustrated
after hours
& falls into me
bearing aromatic kisses
it relaxes me
nights
when I'm afraid
the loud dizzy lady upstairs
is finally going to topple
down thru the ceiling
or at least snap
& pitch the fit
we've all felt coming

A DANCE FOR LI PO

2 lbs bananas
2 rootbeers
4 McIntosh apples
(best of the little ones
which is all that was left)
orange juice
corn
halibut
2 dollars & something
a quick peek inside the bookstore
surrounded by the uppermiddleclass
housewives in expensive boots
hubbies in expensive beards
children got up like film urchins
in funny hats
funny heads

The sky thickens
all the lights come on
I drag it all home
sniffle in the cold
cut across the playground
where kids're chasing after
flies they cant even see
wink at the inevitable moon anyway
have another go at the mailbox

exhale
take my place at the door
come in laughing at the musty corners
dig into the bag
take it all out
stack it all up
sing over the bananas

stand there
just paying visits

to all the good places
Ive been over the years
trying out the different kinds
of darkness
& light
myself but a shadow
on the world wall
unpriced
unbought

gone today
here tomorrow

DANCING TOGETHER

Already it's been years
since you surprised me
from the noonday shadows
of my cheap pension
with its empty wine bottles
& sad scrubbed balconies
in a Madrid that long ago
went the way of Moorish ballads
dime romances
upright pianos painted black &
trimmed in lace,
or the red & yellow quivering
of flowers on a hillside
as military aircraft
zooms overhead

Surrounding one another
we swayed in the rickety hallway
laughing at the top of the stairs
like a couple of sweating

hundred dollar gypsies
re-united by an old deep song,
working our helpless magic
one upon the other
word against word
silence against silence,
sorcerers on welfare

Again I await
& go looking for you
in the shadow of this new night
in which I would bury
the blueness of my thoughts
& my troublesome words
like a musician
after the engagement
packs his instruments away
& encases himself
in the warm dark folds
of a woman's love

A DANCE FOR MA RAINEY

I'm going to be just like you, Ma
Rainey this monday morning
clouds puffing up out of my head
like those balloons
that float above the faces of white people
in the funnypapers

I'm going to hover in the corners
of the world, Ma
& sing from the bottom of hell
up to the tops of high heaven
& send out scratchless waves of yellow

& brown & that basic black honey
misery

I'm going to cry so sweet
& so low
& so dangerous,
Ma,
that the message is going to reach you
back in 1922
where you shimmer
snaggle-toothed
perfumed &
powdered
in your bauble beads

hair pressed & tied back
throbbing with that sick pain
I know
& hide so well
that pain that blues
jives the world with
aching to be heard
that downness
that bottomlessness
first felt by some stolen delta nigger
swamped under with redblooded american agony;
reduced to the sheer shit
of existence
that bred
& battered us all,
Ma,
the beautiful people
our beautiful brave black people
who no longer need to jazz
or sing to themselves in murderous vibrations
or play the veins of their strong tender arms
with needles
to prove we're still here

DANCING IN THE STREET

for my NYC summer workshop students

Just because you wear a natural baby
dont mean you aint got a processed mind.
The field is open
the whole circle of life
is ours for the jumping into,
we ourselves the way we feel
right now
re-creating ourselves
to suit particular dreams & visions
that are no one else's.

Who needs that big mortgaged house
those household finance cars
they advertise
so scientifically
between newscasts,
expensive fronts
those foot-long cigarettes
that brand of breath?

I'd have to travel all the way
back to Lemuria
(cradle of the race
beneath the Pacific)
to bring back a more golden picture of us
the way we looked today
the way we are all the time inside,
healthy black masters
of our own destiny;
set at last on slashing the reins
& shaking off the blinders
that keep the north american
trillion dollar mule team
dragging its collective ass
into that nowhere desert
of bleached white bones & bomb tests.

DANCE OF THE INFIDELS

in memory of Bud Powell

The smooth smell of Manhattan taxis,
Parisian taxis, it doesnt matter, it's
the feeling that modern man is all youve
laid him out to be in those tinglings & rushes;
the simple touch of your ringed fingers
against a functioning piano.

       The winds of Brooklyn
still mean a lot to me. The way certain chicks
formed themselves & their whole lives around
a few notes, an attitude more than anything.
I know about the being out of touch, bumming
nickels & dimes worth of this & that off
him & her here & there — everything but
hither & yon.

    Genius does not grow on trees.

          I owe
you a million love dollars & so much more than
thank-you for re-writing the touch & taste & smell
of the world for me those city years when I could
very well have fasted on into oblivion.

        Ive just
been playing the record you made in Paris with Art
Blakey & Lee Morgan. The european audience
is applauding madly. I think of what Ive heard
of Buttercup's flowering on the Left Bank & days
you had no one to speak to. Wayne Shorter is
beautifying the background of sunlight with
children playing in it & shiny convertibles
& sedans parked along the block as I blow.

                                                            Grass
grows. Negroes. Women walk. The world, in case
youre losing touch again, keeps wanting the same
old thing.

          You gave me some of it; beauty I sought
before I was even aware how much I needed it.

                                              I know
this world is terrible & that one must, above all,
hold onto the heart & the hearts of others.

                        I love *you*

THE JOHN COLTRANE DANCE

Fly on into my poem
Mr Love Trane —

I know the air isnt all that green
but the sound the sound
the sound above all else
hovering there
vibrating my chair
making the tree dance
the sunrise astound,
the sound surrounds us

— the Alabama surge,
Little Rock,
Philadelphia P.A.
(where that sound must have smoothed stones
& cleansed the veins of many a Quaker);

hurt song,
the tag-along

(I know sound cures)

In this fickle sea
of sound
that churns in waves
on all the sides of my becoming,
let the song be you,
Mr Love Trane —

In this long day of spirit
let song be night
& the showering of notes
stars in that beloved firmament

MYSELF WHEN I AM REAL

for Charles Mingus

The sun is shining in my backdoor
right now.
           I picture myself thru jewels
the outer brittleness gone as I
fold within always.   Melting.

Love of life is love of God
sustaining all life,
                  sustaining me
when wrong or un-self-righteous
in drunkenness & in peace.
                  He who loves me
is me. I shall return to Him always,
my heart is rain, my brain earth,

my heart is rain, my brain earth,
but there is only one sun & forever
it shines forth one endless poem
of which my ranting, my whole life
is but breath.

          I long to fade back
into this door of sun forever

DANCING

     1

Yes the simplicity of my life
is so complicated,
on & on it goes,
my lady is gone,
she's at work by now
pulling that 4 to midnight shift.
The hours pass,
I make passes at sumptuous shapes
(typewritten you know)
& rediscover that the Muse is a bitch,
any muse,
music
comes into the picture.
I should be out having adventures
like all the other authors
chasing down dialogue
in the fashionable ghettos,
spearing the bizarre,
everything but falling deeper & deeper
into bad habits
into debt
into traps

in to love
in love
in love with strangers.

I couldve been a trench-coated pusher
& dealt heroin to diplomats
or stood around looking innocent enough
& landed up in the dexamil chewinggum nights
with some of the Go-Go girls who really know
Sun Frun Cisco,
like the time you had to lead me around like a sister
& buy me hangover sandwiches;
I went banging into one pay phone after another
& emptied out musta been a good 6 bucks in coins
all toll
& we did a little laughing of our own
on the benches.

But getting by in Never-Never Land is never enough.
Life is more than fun & games.
The thought
after all
that either of us is capable of being assassinated
at any moment
for absolutely nothing
& relatively little
is of course unnerving.
The clouds of blue summer
keep getting whiter & thicker
by the afternoon
especially up around the mountains
but nobody cares
in California
nobody dares.

Ladies & gentlemen keep sitting down
at the same old exquisite harpsichords;
bluesmen keep hanging around recording studios
for 3 days in a row

trying to get a hit out of there;
blurry-eyed filipinos
with matching wives or irish girlfriends
keep having a go at pizza
in dim lit parlors run by greeks
served up by lackadaisical she-slavs
from the middlewests,
shy wasps out of Bakersfield.

Kids who werent even born
when I first got on to
how completely the Word can kill
& restore
keep practicing up to tangle with the Man;
drunks & soberer citizens
keep trying to sneak free looks
up inside the topless shoeshine stand
on Columbus Ave,
more post-colonial amuricana;
dogs & cats keep checking out pet food commercials
& running up more in vet bills
than my late grayed grandfather
ever earned,
he was a farmer all right
but who isnt
nowadays
we all keep farming one another
into the ground
& steady losing.

Ahhhhhmerica!
you old happy whore
you miserable trigger-happy cowboy
as bound to death as an overweight film harlot
whose asset's begun to drag
& whose hollywood prophets have to put
the bad mouth out
to gentlemen of the board backeast
"It's all over dolling

it's *been* all over."
Pity
how fast the deal can go down
when there's nothing
even speculative
to hold it up.

    2

In the end there are only beautiful things to say.
Never mind how dirty the floor was
or the mind of the Cuban lady across the street
who suspects you of being a filthy drug addict
who heaves stones at his wife every night
& if his house burned down this evening
it wouldnt be any big thing.

There is all this.
There are friends who'll never know
who you really are
& care less;
sick powerful men
in high dizzying places
who do not operate under the influence of music
who would just as soon assassinate
as make a hero of you
once youre no longer capable of
impeding their selfish proposals.
Their children wear sweatshirts
with your face
your hallowed face shines promiscuously
from the fronts of their sweatless children's
T-shirts
& there will be talk of a 6-hour TV spectacular
the combined effort of all the net-
works.
      20th Century–Fox is going to do the picture.
The donations come rolling in.

▾ ▾ ▾

It keeps coming back tho.
Children keep getting themselves born,
the soil that once was sweet to taste
draws up & hardens like cornbread baked too long.
Not a green loving thing emerges.
Our children invade the sea.
Evolving fish
plot revolution
against seething ex-fish
& time is moving it on.

Verily
the power that churns the sea
is a solar delight
a celestial upheaval:
the moon is not the moon we think
but serves.

The moon is your face
in the window of the world
the power heart that pumps beneath
the blood that would splatter every whichway
(as from the bellies of cool slit fish)
coursing to its original destinations
watering insights
bathing our insides
washing the way clear for new origins.

It is inevitable
that we should come to these dark places
to these waters where the drowning
appears to take place &
where attitudes of the ignorant
— our former future selves —
appall us in our journeying forth.
Many's the throat I may have slashed
or angel betrayed

in lives past
out of indignation
thinking it might be one less ass
to contend with
in bringing the promiseland to this planet
here & now
once & for all who counted.

But the knife doubles back
& gets to the point
where environment becomes foul
or the mind has harbored so much pain
that it gives itself up
throws itself away
or collapses
wanting to die
wanting to have been dead
& absent

3

Be the mystic
& wage ultimate revolution,
be true to your self,
be what you always wanted
but be that.

No need to pack up
rush into hiding
& be teaching hypnotism in Harlem
advanced gun-running in Angola
Lima or Port-au-Prince
or be back on 12th Street
dealing in automatics
before the dramatic eye
of national educational television.

Be the taker by surprise
of CIA-subsidized marimba bands &

disconsolate hindu castaways,
be the avowed lover of
nothing-to-lose niggers
thru whom Ive returned to the scene of our crimes
because of whose endurance
& in whose care
I was first able to discern
the forcefulness of living love
magnetized at last
from its hidingplace:
the lie,
the not-for-real.

Be yourself
man
they always warned.
                    Find out
what you really are.
Be that!

4

> *I have busted my gut enough*
> *in this absurd horserace*
> *where the jockeys are thrown*
> *from their saddles*
> *and land among the spectators*
>   Nicanor Parra

Now that some layers have been peeled back
& I can see where dreams I acted out at 15
came true
I want nothing more than
the touch of that peace
the digging for which
has rocked me down thru months & years
of nothing doing
getting nowhere
drinking too much in

drowning too little out
desiring to be infinitely drunk
hiding up under the skirts of women
the soft skin
attracting
as it always does
the hard of seeing
the impossible to touch.

Now that I have walked along envying birds
the security of their placement in nature
& on moment's notice
glanced down toward the sea
on a schedule
that doesnt permit me
time to sit much out;
now that some crystalization of what living's about
has taken place
within
I'm content to settle
for nothing less
than the honey itself.
I have tasted the milk &
found it sour.

Heaven was never more delicious
to me: an earth eater
than when rhythmically presented
the April I met a stranger in a street
a mystic
a prophet
a seeker true enough
with no bullshit attached
who looked honestly into my eyes
& explained to me more than where I'd been
or would have to go;
he touched my trembling hand & hinted
what steps I might take to get there.

Now that I have retraced all the old roads
in this road show version of my past
Ive been putting on
for some time
now
I am ready
to fade out of show biz.

Now that I have risen from the long nap
it is again 7:35 pm
of what this morning
was a lucid new day.
Lights are shining from my window.
Outside
new men & women walk toward one another
in a nighttime field of energy.

Warmblooded &
a little confused
I move toward what I'm hoping is the light.

All my struggles have led me to this moment.

May all your struggles lead likewise toward peace.

Let the revolutions proceed!

DANCING PIERROT

The Chinese moon
I knew it once,
I knew the dusty Egypt moon
& the great snow moon of Mexico
back of Mt. Popocatépetl
lifetimes ago

decades
anybody's moment

I know them now
these fat these skinny moons
that offer just so much of themselves
a piece at a time
for just so long

4 moons
3 moons
2 moons
1 moon these moons
the Tokyo moon
Bahia moon
my San Francisco moon
your Tanzanian moon
pouring its light live
into the orifices of women
& men who work thru the night
in order that they might one day
put themselves down
against its illuminated surfaces
armed to the eyes
with star guns

Mad moon
monkey moon
junior moon
crescent moon of Moors
unmapped moon of mind,

sweet dry wine of light
that I drink
with my eyes!

THE IMITATION DANCE

Time is Berkeley
the place is now
where some unenlightened children
beyond the rim of my attention
are actively lollygagging
on the hard sidewalk
laid in
where trees once loved so informally,
or dribbling Ishmael Reed's zen basketballs
across the playground in windy spring light.
I make nothing of this until the din subsides
& I'm forced to account for the silence.

Orange juice a roll some lettuce banana/milk
the way we eat now, appearances
real enough
dissolving in the juices
of my hidden stomach.
Form *is* emptiness.
                        Objects clutter my vision:
books beads fern shoes machine-parts a table
a decoration squash a
chance scattering of oolong leaf
the 29¢ teacup & pencils
apple seed a fragrant picture of you
pinned against the wall
to mountains
a TV set that's never worked
some clocks,
a moment,
our plastic cubbyhole in Ha Ha Street.

Everything is supposed to have changed yet
flatulence & decline are still being discussed
with the same open passion
in all but the right places;
I manage to stay as poor as ever,

a part-Indian excavator of old inner cities
out here at the edge of the jungle,
but one day I'm going to move
even further from the so-called center
on into the heart of things.

Years may pass again
or only some hours before I dance out
the shape of another clear day,
eternal unit of forever

DANCING IN THE LAUNDROMAT
(or, DUST: AN ORDINARY SONG)

I love you
I need you
you in the laundromat
among the telltale result
of the ubiquitous garment industry
shirts & blouses
(we have arms)
bras & the tops of bathingsuits
(you have breasts)
briefs & shorts panties skirts & bottoms
(we have bottoms centers middles stomachs
bellies crotches & cores)
on down to trousers & slacks
& contemporary leg gear butt-
lined whitelined bluelined
roselined blacklined khaki-
lined rainbow clothesline
line-up —

I blow you clean low kisses
from transparent lips

of vowel-shaped word
& no-word,
the well sudsed stocking-
feet continuing
the beds & sheets
pillowcases
tender towel & rag
apparel we take for granted,
delight of all but the nakedest eye.

What is it we wear
that never needs washing?

What is it we wear
that never wears?

THE DANCER

When white people speak of being uptight
theyre talking about dissolution & deflection
but when black people say uptight
they mean everything's all right.
I'm all right.
The poem brushes gayly past me
on its way toward completion,
things exploding in the background
a new sun
in a new sky
canteloupes & watermelon for breakfast
in the Flamingo Motel
with cousin Inez
her brown face stretching & tightening
to keep control of the situation,
pretty Indian cheeks
cold black wavelets of hair,

her boyfriend
smiling from his suit.
We discuss concentration camps
& the end of time.
My mustache
wet with canteloupe juice
would probably singe
faster than the rest of me
like the feathers of a bird over flame
in final solution of
the Amurkan problem.
Ah, Allah,
that thou hast not forsaken me
is proven by the light
playing around the plastic slats
of half-shut venetian blinds
rattling in this room on time
in this hemisphere on fire.
The descendants of slaves
brush their teeth
adorn themselves before mirrors
speak of peace & of living kindness &
touch one another
intuitively & in open understanding.
"It could be the end of the world,"
she says, "they use to didnt be afraid
of us but now that they are
what choice do they have
but to try & kill us?"
but she laughs & I laugh & he laughs
& the calmness in their eyes
reaches me finally
as I dig my spoon into the belly of a melon

THE ROBBIE'S DANCE

Years later
I fall back in.
The jukebox is new
but the music is dated
the talk is dated
even the beer is dated
but the people are the same;
a black & tan bohemia
that never was,
Miss Brown Baby in a getup
that defines her squareness
right up to the hip,
Mrs Lager Belly
Mr Fare Thee Well &
Mr Ne'er Do Well
walk in
for the thousandth time that day
& stage a talk-in
up near the exit.
I keep trying to grin sincerely
like a liberated bore
but the game's too quick
to be played back
successfully
by my facial muscles.
The chinese jew
who scoops the gravied rice
to go with turkey
or chow mein
has been jaded so long
he's taken to hiding out
backstage in the kitchen
between I.D. checks
to keep his eyelids from atrophying.
The dancers here
are all string-operated
but even the thread is worn & dated.

The john is a living little magazine
a sort of piss wall review
that takes the story up
wherever you leave off.
On my way back out
I'm busy picturing
the illustrious canned hippie
who sticks it out in here for years
before finally typing up &
getting his thesis published on
Current Trends in California

DANCING ALL ALONE

We move thru rooms & down the middle of freeways,
myself & I.
A feeling lumps up in the throat
that says I wont be living forever.
The middle of the month signifies
the end of some beginning
the beginning of some end.
Once I thought the heart could be ripped out
like doll filling
& naked essence examined
but I'm a man
not a mannikin.
I would transfer to the world
my idea of what it's like beneath flesh & fur.
I cannot do this without making fools of myself.
Cold winds whoosh down on me under winter stars
& the way ahead is long but not uncertain.
I am neither prince nor citizen
but I do know what is noble in me
& what is usefully vulgar.
It is from this point that the real radiates.

I move & am moved,
do & am done for.
My prison is the room of myself
& my rejection of both is my salvation,
the way out being the way in,
the freeway that expands to my true touch,
a laughter in the blood that dances.

2 TAKES FROM *LOVE IN LOS ANGELES*

A potted fern
in a Vine St apartment
spreads its green delicate tentacles
like my cousin Cynthia
does her fingers
at the piano
in the window
West 27th St
the colored district
where almost everybody
has a REpublic or a 73-
telephone number;
no maps sold
to the homes of these stars:

my Uncle James
game to the end
in his rickety walkup
room on the 2nd floor
with low-rent view
of rooftops & parkinglots
neon liquor messages
where you watch
a dude out of Texas
with a process

& a redhead
turn left
on a red light &
barely miss
getting his jag
smashed to pieces;
Unc is imagining
how many nickel numbers
he'd have to hit
back in Detroit
to get his used car
overhauled again —

James
Cynthia
Richard
Toni
Marti
Inez
Desi
Pierre,
their blood my blood
in this other kind of colony

way out west

where the Indians are real
& train for equal opportunity positions,

where the young Chicanos
whip ass
& wig behind
soul music &
Brown is Beautiful,
where lithe &
lipsticked Chinese girls
avoid Japanese advances
maintaining that cool
by any means necessary,

where the keeper of dreams
is solemn &
wears a whole body dickey
from odious head
to fabulous toe
to entice the young women
& other boys

In one dream
the third world ghosts
of Charlie Chan &
Mantan Moreland
in the gentle sting
of a gasoline twilight
take turns
kissing on
an unidentified starlet
with a natural &
a bankamericard

▼   ▼   ▼

Even the flourishing nazi
whose children smoke opium
& inject themselves
for laughs
in Orange County
has his angeleno mistresses,
intelligent negresses
in auburn wig
& shades;
strange thin-lipped aryans
whose underwear glitters,
new Marilyn Monroes
in colorfast fashion knits
parking their cars
in puddles of quicksilver
who wink at spooks

propped next to palmtrees
Love licks its lip
at no one

A DANCE FOR AGING HIPSTERS

For the aging hipster
there isnt any cure,
as he fumbles the key
to his own front door
it gives & opens anyway

Loaded again yes
it's him & he's loaded again
this time on time but
the very mellowness he fathered
& nurtured thru high spring
has fallen now
into an earlier autumn
than even he
had anticipated

Dreamily he clings
to his favorite memories
of splendid explosions
that titillated the glands,
cold implosions
in the blue of his heart
& he suffers leftover visions
of festive backrooms
on crazy warm nights
where he jived other jivers
& set the pace
for a whole nervous subculture
strung out behind loneliness

DEAR ARL

Sweets you were glittering this morning
brushing your teeth with no more Crest
& me lying there need to get up
grouching in the form of my self stupid

You just said what you had to say
& let me go my way complaining about
shirts & cooking which I dont really care about
hardly even think about really except
to happy music in the afternoon awake

Well I got the money & bought some books
& had a cheeseburger & dish of beans at Kip's
with Tom Glass who put me in a good mood
talking about people making comebacks —
"What a sad scene a cat who has to think
                    in those terms even
as if to say I'm in style now folks but
                    watch out
I'm subject to fade out any minute now"

I'd change her sad rags into glad rags
                if I could
sing The Four Seasons on KYA radio twelve sixty
                San Fran Cisco —
Youre taking the F bus to the city tonight
straight from work to buy another pretty
for your wardrobe still growing 2 dresses now
& I have to be in show biz at The Jabberwock
for $17.50 which is current union scale
                Wow!

Redbeans & rice on stove & squash coming up,
no idea whether youll like the dinner —

I think of you alone picking over nylons
& slips & sweet little sweaters on sale,

moving up Grant Ave with that special switch
which isnt really a switch at all but your self
            walking

I like your walk & taste & your dresses,
also the way you counter my crabbiness,
            yes —
then too I love you & all the rest of it

FOR KENNETH & MIRIAM PATCHEN

Here
I am cutting you
these fresh healthy flowers
from my sick bed
where I toss with nickel illuminations.
Time is a fever
that burns in the pores
consuming everything the mind creates.
I send you
this cool arrangement of dream blossoms
these tender stems & shining leaves
while I shiver
& detect in your own eyes
of gentle remove
a similar disgust with what has come
to our fat cancerous land
of the sensual circus
& the disembodied broadcast wave,
swallowing in sorrow
to hear the old hatred
& undercover selfishness
rumbling back up from the bosoms of men
out into the good open air.
May these new flowers

from the forest of my heart
bring you a breath of the joy
men must believe they are going to recover
by moving again & again
against one another.

LEMONS, LEMONS

Hanging from fresh trees
or yellow against green
in a soft blaze of afternoon
while I eat dutifully
my cheese & apple lunch
or the coolness of twilight
in some of these California towns
I inhabited a lifetime ago

Hung that way
filled up with sunlight
like myself ripe with light
brown with light & ripe with shadow
the apple red & gold & green with it
cheese from the insides of
sun-loving cows

Sweet goldenness of light
& life itself
sunny at the core
lasting all day long
into night
into sleep
permeating dream shapes
forming tingly little words
my 2¢ squeezed out
photosynthetically

in hasty praise
of lemon/light

PARIS

I couldnt ever tell you
just what might have been going on,
the gray brick nowhereness
of certain gendarmes
if you can dig it

But for now
you follow me into ice cream places
where they push hamburgers
& beer too
where nothing seems to have changed
since Worcester,
where I can feel the flirtiness
of meat heat rising in the streets,
a european princess
easing herself up next to me
dead on the Champs Elysées
I buy my *jetons*
& make phonecalls like a nice fellow
to whom directions are mapped out sweetly
by tender old ladies born in Rue La Bruyere
as all the african brothers
hop on & off the metro
jammed up with birds & algerians

England no
this is France
another colonial power environment
far from Richard Wright's
or my own wrong Mississippi

Encircled by luminous space
I lay my woolly head
against your tan belly of Italy
& listen to the fat cars in the streets
hometown of the bourgeoisie
& clean creamy ladies & you
sparkle darkly
where I too
am pregnant
with astonishment

READING NIJINSKY'S DIARY

for JoAnne

Who of us is not mad

I am set loose again
Moved beyond tears
by perfect utterance
— cut loose, freed
to know ever for all
as I did so perfectly
long ago & all ways
that poem story book
all play on nothing
if not skin
to house truths
spurting up no where

I have been ragged
hair uncombable
licking sour lips
mounting floor heat
that it may rise

up my slept-in limbs

Morning explodes
behind my eyes,
I dance out into a rain
forest of bodily concern,
vine-tangled nerve
crash & trip into
sweet leaf trees
to teach me roots
& branches of becoming

Becoming receptor of
Life Death & Feeling
you need only speak,
"My madness is my love
for mankind," for me
to be sane again

POEM FOUND EMPTYING OUT MY POCKETS

for Ron & Taffy Dahl

It is a normal day.
I rise just as the room's filling up again
with light
feeling myself to be the award winning goof-off
who wanted to practice yoga
& write the world a thousand good books
simultaneously,
whose lady is slumbering in Massachusetts
lit up & pounding with dream horses.

An orange fur creature taps me naked
purring for breakfast
(groaning for roast fowl or ocean fish).

Re-washing
I think things over
then re-dress & re-comb with my African woodcomb.
I consume oranges bananas & cold milk
yearning to know more about fruits & animals.

Out in the streets I know everybody
but I dont know anything.
I dont know these blind buildings.
I dont know what people are doing.
I dont even know what I'm doing.
I arrive at my job,
the sun makes its round,
at noon if it's warm I sleep under a tree,
at midnight sometimes trees sleep under me,
angels beckon from books & at stop/lights,
the mouths of warmongers work overtime
to convince me I am what I'm not,
fingers touch my palm making change
or I stutter
greeting somebody I havent seen.

Behind everyone's eye
I can sense the steady stream of dreams
or temporary malice
rippling & flickering helplessly.
Who needs television?
I could tell everything
if there werent so many of us.

A little dinner
a little nourishment
a little remembrance of things to come
a considerate voice against my cheek &
I too am willing to continue

wearily inspired by this strange change
called love
that keeps coming
like death
to everybody

A LITTLE MORE TRAVELING MUSIC

A country kid in Mississippi I drew water
    from the well
& watched our sun set itself down behind
    the thickets,
hurried from galvanized baths to hear music
over the radio — Colored music, rhythmic & electrifying,
more Black in fact than politics & flit guns.

Mama had a knack for snapping juicy fruit gum
& for keeping track of the generations of chilrens
she had raised, reared & no doubt forwarded,
rising thankfully every half past daybreak
to administer duties the poor must look after
if theyre to see their way another day, to eat, to live.

▼   ▼   ▼

I lived & upnorth in cities sweltered & froze,
    got jammed up & trafficked
in everybody's sun going down but took up with the
    moon
as I lit about getting it all down up there
    where couldnt nobody knock it out.

Picking up slowly on the gists of melodies, most noises
    softened.
I went on to school & to college too, woke up cold

[51]

& went my way finally, classless, reading all poems,
    some books & listening to heartbeats.

Well on my way to committing to memory the ABC
    reality,
I still couldnt forget all that motherly music,
those unwatered songs of my babe-in-the-wood days
until, committed to the power of the human voice,
I turned to poetry & to singing by choice,
reading everyone always & listening, listening for a
    silence deep enough
to make out the sound of my own background music.

BIRTHDAY POEM

First light of day in Mississippi
son of laborer & of house wife
it says so on the official photostat
not son of fisherman & child fugitive
from cottonfields & potato patches
from sugarcane chickens & well-water
from kerosene lamps & watermelons
mules named jack or jenny & wagonwheels,

years of meaningless farm work
work Work WORK WORK WORK —
"Papa pull you outta school bout March
to stay on the place & work the crop"
— her own earliest knowledge
of human hopelessness & waste

She carried me around nine months
inside her fifteen year old self
before here I sit numbering it all

How I got from then to now
is the mystery that could fill a whole library
much less an arbitrary stanza

But of course you already know about that
from your own random suffering
& sudden inexplicable bliss

IT IS GOD THAT MOVES IN YOUR HEART

You turn on your pillow
in the Chinese new year
& breathe the hour into my face
your dream eyes fluttering
in the gas heat
of our clock room
with its stuffed bed
& its loneliness.
Beyond these walls
trees are stretching
& shaking themselves
in the automatic drizzle
of yesterday continuing.
Refusing to rise
& bathe & meditate
I groan on my boney side
like an unreflecting animal
planted like vegetable
& lazy as mineral
watching you smile out
from secret film shadows
backstage of some paradise
I would gladly invade

The Song Turning Back into Itself
(1971)

I don't know if you have been away,
I go to bed with you, & I wake up with you.
In my dreams you are beside me.
If the earrings of my ears tremble
I know it is you moving in my heart.

Nahuatl Indian Song / Poem
(Mexico)

LONELINESS

The poet is the dreamer.
He dreams that the clock stops
& 100 angels wandering wild
drift into his chamber
where nothing has been settled

Should he get himself photographed
seated next to a mountain
like Chairman Mao
the real sun flashing golden
off his real eyes
like the light off stones
by oceans?

Give me your perfect hand
& touch me simply with a word,
one distillation of forever

Should he put his white tie on
with his black shirt
& pass himself off as a docile gangster
for the very last time?

The poet's dream is real
down to the last silver bullet
Should he slip again to Funland
in the city & throw dimes down holes
to watch hungry women flicker
one hair at a time
in kodacolor
from sad civilized boxes?

Should he practice magic
on politicians &
cause them to crack their necks
in a laughing fit?

The poet is the dreamer.
He dreams babies asleep in wombs
& counts the wasted sighs
lost in a flake of dusty semen
on a living thigh

Should he dream the end of an order,
the abolition of the slave trade,
the restoration to life
of dead millions
filing daily past time clocks
dutifully gorging themselves
on self-hatred & emptiness?

Should he even dream
an end to loneliness,
the illusion that
we can do without
& have no need
of one another?

It is true that he needs you,
I need you,
I need your pain & magic,
I need you now more than ever
in every form & attitude —
gesturing with a rifle in your hand
starving in some earthly sector
or poised in heavenly meditation
listening to the wind
with the third ear
or staring into forever
with the ever-watchful third eye,
you are needed

The poet is the dreamer
the poet is himself the dream
& in this dream
he shares your presence

Should he smash down walls
& expose the ignorance
beneath our lying noisiness?

No! No!
the gunshot he fires
up into the silent air
is to awaken

FRIDAY THE 12TH

Floating thru morning
    I arrive at afternoon
& see the bright lightness
    light ness
    of it all

& thank God
& go on living
taking spoiled strawberries
& a tapioca pudding gone bad
    out the ice box

Must wash my hair &
    go get it cut off my head
    head itches
Notice my luck changes
    when I've had
    a hair cut
same as if I dont rise before noon
    the day doesnt go right

Afternoon becomes evening becomes night

There're worlds into worlds between all worlds
    so dont worry
    about divisions of day
for even when I fall out asleep the day
    wont have ended
    wont have begun

In fact years whoosh by in time for me
        to see myself as endless fool child
& to learn better than
    to laugh at such conditions

Now I bathe & go out into the streets
    airplane raging overhead
    (your head perhaps)
    reminding me how
    even floating must come to an end

EROSONG

I first saw you in a trance
(you were in the trance, not me).
Me I was dancing

on turbulent waters.
All my shores had been pulled up
& naked I was nowhere

but there was some drowsy grace you offered,
some rendezvous from way-back to be fulfilled.
I moved toward you

saying everything,
you nothing.
The 20th Century moon

did its turn-around,
revealing how much the sun it was
in the face of your light,

all that light,
in the daytime,
at night

THE OLD FASHIONED CINCINNATI BLUES

for Jesse "Lone Cat" Fuller

O boy the blues!
I sure do love blues
but the blues dont like me

This is Cincinnata Ohia 1949
& that's me & my brother Frank
in the NY Central Train Station
trying to get it together
on our way down
to Meridian Mississippi
where later I hid
in cornfields, smoked butts &
dreamed all about
the sunny grownup future,
dreamed about Now

Ah but that Now that
Right Now that is,
all I wanna dream about's

that NY Cincy Terminal
that summer with its intervals
of RC Cola Coolers,
tin tub baths taken
one at a time
back behind the evening stove —

Chickens —

Our grandmother
(Mrs Lillian Campbell) —

Cousin George & Uncle John
swapping ghost stories
Saturday nite —

O Americana!
United Statesiana!

A lonesome high,
a funnytime cry,
the blues
the blues
the blues

THE PROBLEM OF IDENTITY

Used to identify with my father first making me want to be a
    gas station attendant simple drink coca-cola listen to the
    radio, work on people's cars, hold long conversations in the
    night black that clean gas smell of oil & no-gas, machine
    coolness, rubber, calendars, metal sky, concrete, the bearing
    of tools, the wind — true Blue labor Red & White

Identified with Joe Louis: Brown Bomber, you know They'd
    pass along the mud streets of Laurel Mississippi in loud

speaker truck, the white folks, down by where the colored
schools was & all of us, out there for Recess or afterschool
are beckoned to come get your free picture of Joe Louis,
C'mon & get it kids it's Free, c'mon naow — What it is is
chesterfield cigarettes in one corner of the beautiful slick
photo of Mr. Louis is the blurb, *Joe like to smoke too, see, and
he want all yall to follow right long in his footsteps & buy up
these here chesterfields & smoke your little boodies off & youll be
able to step up in that ring begloved & punch a sucker out.* It
was the glossiness of the photo, I finally figured out years
later, that had me going — didnt really matter whose
picture was on it altho it was nice to've been Joe's because
he was about as great as you could get downsouth, post
world war II as the books say

Identified with Otis (think his name was) worked at grocery
store in Ocean Springs, came by, would sit & draw on pieces
of brown paperbag, drew in 1940s style of cartoons
bordering on "serious" sketching, i.e., in the manner of
those sultan cartoons with the harem gals by that black
cartoonist E. Campbell Sims you see em all the time in old
Esquires & Playboys Well, that's the way Otis could draw &
he'd show me in the make-do livingroom seated on do-fold
how to do a portrait of a chic perfect anglo-featured woman,
say, in profile out of his head built mostly from magazine &
picture-show impressions, & he could draw lots of world
things, drew me for instance

Later Otis went up to Chicago, sadness, madness, wed, bled,
dope, hopeless, catapulted into the 20th Century like the
rest of us — rudely,
                         steeped in homemade makeshift
chemical bliss of/or flesh, waiting for nothing less than The
Real Thing

PACHUTA, MISSISSIPPI/A MEMOIR

I too
once lived
in the country

    Incandescent
        fruits
        in moonlight
    whispered to me
        from trees
        of
        1950
    swishing
    in the green nights

            wavelengths away
                from
            tongue-red meat
            of melon

        wounded squash
        yellow as old afternoons

        chicken
            in love
            with calico
    hiss & click of flit gun

    juice music
        you suck up
    lean stalks of field cane

            Cool as sundown
            I lived there too

FOR JOANNE IN POLAND

You are not to trouble yourself
with your ladyness
your blackness,
mysteries
of having been brought up
on collard greens
      bagels
              &
                  Chef Boy-Ar-Dee

Nor must you let the great haters
of our time
rattle in your heart

They are small potatoes
whose old cries
for blood
may be heard
any afternoon of the millennium
any portion
      of this
              schoolroom globe

OLD LIGHT

How quickly morphology
    shifts
        the whole landscape
      thrice uprooted
        all the tall redwoods
      yanked & shipped to Japan
        since you snapped
          that one

My eyes grow new
    the smile crookeder —
        Here your coloring
      shines out of you differently
        as tho measured thru
      some other kind of prism
        one by which the wavelength
           of a smile
        is easily recorded

Like distant hills by moonlight
    your own dark beauty
        brightens
    like meanings of remembered places
        illuminated
           by time & distance

           Carmel Valley
           the Zoo at the end
               of the Judah line
           Tomales Bay
           McGee Street
           Smith Grade Road
           Avenida Cinco de Mayo
           Guadalajara Guadalajara
           the beach at Point Reyes of
               saying goodbye
         to sand the ocean the untakeable
           sea breeze
               doorway
                 backyard
                 garden
               alleyway
            bench
           forest of countryside city

The passing of time will
        shatter your heart
            recorded in
        mute shadow & light
            the photographer's hour

THE SONG TURNING BACK INTO ITSELF 1

I sing folk tunes unrhymed.
With my heart keeping the beat,
Trust your sorrow, then, to my bosom
Where it will find its cure.

Li Chin-fa

Breathing in morning
breezing thru rainbows
vanishing in my own breath mist,
how can I still not feel
this warm beat of beats
my own heart of hearts,

myself: an articulate colored boy
who died lucky
who wouldve kept talking himself
into dying,
creatively of course,
the soulful touch
pulsing thru his nervous system
like light thru the arteries of trees,

that mystified young man
whose stupidity knew no bounds
& at whose touch
gold shriveled to tinfoil
wine gurgled into faucet water,

[67]

a firstclass fuckup
who but for divine mercy
would have gone
out of commission
long ago
would have become
the original loveboat
cracked up against rocks
in fog or funk,

the rocks in his hard nappy head
the fog in his big blind eyes
the funk in his & everyone's blood
held in
waiting,

waiting

THE SONG TURNING BACK INTO ITSELF 2

a song for little children

Always it's either
a beginning
or some end:
the babys being born
or its parents are
dying, fading on
like the rose
of the poem
withers, its light going out
while gardens come in
to bloom

Let us stand on streetcorners
in the desolate era
propose a new kind
of crazyness

Let us salute one another
one by one
two by two
the soft belly
moving toward
the long sideburns
the adams apple
or no apple at all

Let there be
in this crazyness
a moon
a violin
a drum

Let the beautiful brown girl
join hands with
her black sister
her golden sister
her milkskinned sister
their eternal wombs
turning with the moon

Let there be a flute
to squeal above
the beat & the bowing
to open us up
that the greens
the blues
the yellows
the reds
the silvers &
indescribable rusts
might flow out

amazingly
& blend
with the wind

Let the wobbly spin
of the earth
be a delight
wherein
a caress forms
the most perfect circle

Let the always be love
the beginning be love
love the only
possible
end

THE SONG TURNING BACK INTO ITSELF 3

Ocean Springs Missippy
you dont know about that
unless youve died in magnolia
tripped across the Gulf
& come alive again
or fallen in the ocean
lapping up light
like the sun digging
into the scruffy palm leaves
fanning the almighty trains
huffing it choo-choo
straight up our street
morning noon & nighttrain
squalling that moan
like a big ass blues man
smoking up the sunset

Consider the little house
of sunken wood
in the dusty street
where my father would
cut his fingers
up to his ankles
in fragrant coils
of lumber shavings
the backyard of nowhere

Consider Nazis & crackers
on the some stage
splitting the bill

Affix it all to
my memory of Ma
& her love of bananas
the light flashing
in & out of our lives
lived 25¢ at a time
when pecans were in season
or the crab & shrimp
was plentiful enough
for the fishermen
to give away for gumbo
for o soft hullo
if you as a woman
had the sun in your voice
the wind over your shoulder
blowing the right way
at just that moment in history

THE SONG TURNING BACK INTO ITSELF 4

I violinize peace
in the Nazi era;
semen-colored doves
perched atop sea trains
from the decks of which
women are singing
anti-death songs;
magnificent birds
flop in & out
of tonal pictures
before disappearing
into the green
the blue
the rolling white
of an oceanic music

Tipping thru this skylight
along rooftops
to snuggle in
quaintly
with paintable pigeons
I can still feel
the red & white
the blood sonata
cello'd from me
bow against bone
finger pluck of flesh
as
    I
      laugh
           colors
into your warm wet mouth

▼ ▼ ▼

Behold dogcatchers
the lady watchers
the simple twist of hip
as it cuts electric air
bringing endless delight

I would walk you up trees
& inscribe at the tops
in leaves
these very words
Let us change the design
of their celluloid architecture
into a shape where love could live
(in street Spanish & Swahili)

▼　▼　▼

This music is real

Feel the rhythm

the lips

Feel today

vibrating

in the throat

Feel sound

Feel space

O feel the presence of

light

brighter than distant circuses

in the child night

of the soul

THE SONG TURNING BACK INTO ITSELF 5

The song skips around
The song jumps
like a little boy
leaps a mud puddle

I park in rainlight
I run out of rhymes
I splash thru the puddle
I land in a change
for 10 years seem like
water be rolling
off my back
one bead at a time
but with light
in the center of
every single one

The song sings new images
variations on the theme
of human love &
its shadow
loneliness
(Billie Holiday
mightve been busy
feeding on nuances &
loving a man but
she wouldve understood,
understanding being
the only honorable escape
in the end)

Sing me shadows
Sing me puddles
Sing me rain
Sing me holidays & nights
Sing me holiness
Sing me loneliness

Sing me a skip & a jump
    across a thousand years

But dont sing love,

    just signal

THE SONG TURNING BACK INTO ITSELF 6

terrestrial blues

Again
who am I?
Certainly not the boy
I started out to be
nor the man
nor the poet

Sometimes
alone & saddened
(which is to say joyous)
I get glimpses of myself
the eternal spirit
floating from flower
to tree to grasshopper,
thru whole herds of cattle

I become the skies,
the very air itself —
Me: all things
Me: nothing

It would confuse me
if I didnt know
these lbs. of meat

[75]

bearing the name
my people gave me
to be simply
every body's condition

My soul
knows no name,
no home in being

My soul
seeks your soul

Let us laugh
each at the other
& be friends

THE SONG TURNING BACK INTO ITSELF 7

the fly-away song

Get that feeling sometimes
that
you-cant-hold-me-down
feeling

Wanna shatter
into
ten thousand fragments of emotion —

Splinter!

Rise
above this quivering concrete world
& go sailing thru beds & minds

Sail
higher
&
HIGHER

Crazy that way

SING
one sweet long song to undo
all sickness & suffering
down there on the ground . . .
one huge human gust of insight
& forgiveness

SOARING
over rooftops with
Chagall's chickens

ALIVE

WAKING!

THE PRESTIDIGITATOR 1

What you gonna do when they burn your barrelhouse down?
What you gonna do when they burn your barrelhouse down?
Gonna move out the piano & barrelhouse on the ground.
traditional Afro-American blues

A prestidigitator makes things disappear,
vanish, not unlike a well-paid bookkeeper
or tax consultant or champion consumer

The poet is a prestidigitator, he makes
your old skins disappear & re-clothes you

in sturdy raiment of thought, feeling, soul,
dream & happenstance. Consider him villain of
the earthbound, a two-fisted cowboy with
pencil in one hand & eraser in the other

dotting the horizon of your heart with cool
imaginary trees but rubbing out more than he
leaves in for space so light can get thru

THE PRESTIDIGITATOR 2

I draw hats on rabbits, sew women back
together, let fly from my pockets flocks of
vibratory hummingbirds. The things Ive got

up my sleeve would activate the most listless
of landscapes (the cracked-earth heart of a bigot,
say) with pigeons that boogaloo, with flags that

light up stabbed into the brain. Most of all it's
enslaving mumbo-jumbo that I'd wipe away, a trick
done by walking thru mirrors to the other side

KISS

Mayakovsky was right
The brass of my tuba does blacken
as I oompah & twist down nights

even the best female poets
couldnt brighten with song,

a quiet dog barking distantly
my only excuse for being alive
so late past 12 by taxi
horn & radio in the rain

finally having made it
to the middle of nowhere,
toes aching from the walk
but fingers intact & head
quite nicely on some other planet
where there're no tempting images

to soften the Indian in me,
no sudden left turns or halts
on roads not marked for traffic,

my women human beings being human
who touch my body with a silence
that electrifies like poetry

Mexico, 1969

THE CURATIVE POWERS OF SILENCE

Suddenly
I touch upon wordlessness,
I who watch Cheryl
the blind girl who lives up the street
walking at night
when she thinks no one's looking
deliberately heading into hedges & trees
in order to hug them
& to be kissed,
thus are we each
hugged & kissed.

Wordless
I fill up
listening for nothing
for nothing at all

as when in so-called life
I am set shivering with warmth
by a vision
with the eyes closed
of the Cheryl in me
when I think no one's looking,
plopped down in a field of grass
under watchful trees
letting the pre-mind dream
of nothing at all
nothing at all
no flicker
no shadow
no voice
no cry,

not even dreaming

— being dreamed

YES, THE SECRET MIND WHISPERS

for Bob Kaufman

Poetry's a tree
forever at your door
neither scratching nor
knocking but everywhere
eager to force its way
into the soft warm room

of your ornery old heart,
   slipping
  its fat pink tongue
     into sensitive linings
   of your weary young ear

A tree bearing blossoms, a flower
surfacing in a canal of blood,
the dream auto with dream motor
that idles eternally but has
no moving parts, no fumes just
fragrances beneficial to breathe

It breathes mystery this tree
     but no more so
    than moons over midnight seas
   or the breast of a woman/child
      to whom menstruation's happening
       for the first time

It's the practice of yoga
  on rainy nights in cities,
    the sudden thought of death
     halfway thru dessert, a
  magic wafer you take
     into your mouth
      &
   swallow for dear life

SUNDAY ILLUMINATION

Ive found peace & it's good sleeping late today — head full of
    eternal ideas, eternal emptiness; Phil Elwood jazz on KPFA,
    my wife sunny in tattered red skirt & sea blue T shirt on
    back yard grass getting her Spanish lesson

"How would I say: Friday I went to a party & heard some good
    gospel music?" — & I try to explain the preterite & the im-
    perfect perfectly WHEW! but keep interrupting her with
    poems & to watch a young bee zero in on flaming fuchsia
    branches, wondering if flower & insect survive ex-lives

Then we go hiking in the Berkeley hills first time all year since
    Europe, marriage, satori in the slums — New houses have
    sprung up, split-level clutter; a half finished trap is going up
    on the spot top of Dwight Way where we'd sit on a pile of
    lumber for panoramic vista of Berkeley Oakland Alcatraz in
    the Bay & dazzling San Francisco in the sun — What was it
    like here before the invasions?

So by now I got to pee & head aches from heat & climb & hot-
    dogs we bought & ate walking for breakfast, foul fare — no
    place to sit — Some affluent dogs in heat trail us round a
    bend — the old motorcycle trail looks dangerously uninter-
    esting, guys go up there scrambling & fall — My shirt's
    sticking to my sweat & the friends we thought we'd drop in
    on, whatve we to say to them after all?

Descending Arden Steps I make water on a bush, she covering
    for me — humorous taboo — then comes our pause on the
    stone bench where we almost ruled out wedlock that
    torturous fall twilight of long ago Campanile carrillon woe

Time to count our blessings as in my heart all pain ceases & for
    the longest moment all day I see my sad funny self on earth
    & the gentle terror of her female soul, beautiful, but we're
    alive NOW accumulating karma, no time to hide in places
    — no place to hide in time.

DREAM TAKE: 22

Some old Mexico Lisbon set
rainy at night & shimmery.
I alone flop around in midnight,
see everything from angel angle.

New moonless couples mourn by
arm in arm & all hands
after evenings of being quiet,
for soon whatever's to happen's

happened already, always has.
I smile out over the situation
to keep their tears to myself,
tired of time & so much in need of

this mirage of lovers parading.
Safe, I can sense that I'm soon to
awake with no possible camera
to record what I just saw asleep

APRIL BLUE

It's time the clock got thrown out the window
& the difference between waking & sleeping
be left undeclared, unassumed.
                                It's the
heart's turn to do a few spins in its fluid.
It's time the birds that play in the street
(that you had to slow down for this morning)
flew into your machine & introduced themselves.

It's time you silenced the radio, the stereo,
the TV, the tea kettle, the kettle drum &

flew to where the inner ear beckons, where
closed eyes have always tingled to take you,
to the end of space if necessary, to the place
the horizon's always promised, to a glowing
spirit world where you'd as soon eat as not,
as soon drink as not, as soon make love as not,
as soon be water as air, as soon be moon as sun.

It's time you made yourself beautiful again,
spreading like color in every direction,
rising & rising to every occasion.
                                    Summer
may be coming in, maybe not, this painful year.

Spring is the thing that your window frames now.

It's time you soaked in the new light & laughed.

GROUPIE

Evening isnt so much a playland as it is
a rumpus room, a place where harmony
isnt always complementary & where
spaces between palmtrees of the heart
arent always so spread out.

                        By 3 A.M.
there's love in her hose for the sailor
of saxophones or guitars & she'll try & take
the whole night into her skilled mouth
as tho that were the lover she really wanted
to rub against when all the time true love
inhabits her own fingernails & unshaven body.

You love her for the mental whore she is,
the clothed sun in Libra, the horny sister
who with her loose hair flying can get
no better attention for the time being

ONE WEST COAST

for Gordon Lapides

Green is the color of everything
that isnt brown, the tones ranging
like mountains, the colors changing.

You look up toward the hills & fog —
the familiarity of it after so many years
    a resident tourist.

                A young man walks
toward you in vague streetcrossing denims
& pronounced boots. From the pallor of
    his gait, the orange splotch twin gobs of sunset
    in his shades, from the way he vibrates
    his surrounding air, you can tell, you can tell
        he's friendly, circulating,

            he's a Californian: comes to visit,
                stays for years, marries, moves a wife in,
            kids, wears out TV sets, gets stranded on
                            loneliness,
                    afternoon pharmaceutica,
                so that the sky's got moon in it by
                3 o'clock, is blooo, is blown —

                    The girls: theyre all
            winners reared by grandmothers & CBS.

Luckier ones get in a few dances with
mom, a few hours, before dad goes back
in the slam, before "G'bye I'm off
to be a singer!" & another runaway
Miss American future drifts
over the mountain &
into the clouds.

Still
there's a beautifulness about California.
It's based on the way each eyeblink toward
the palms & into the orange grove leads backstage
into the onionfields.

Unreachable, winter happens inside you.

Your unshaded eyes dilate at the spectacle.

You take trips to contain the mystery.

LONESOME IN THE COUNTRY

How much of me is sandwiches radio beer?
How much pizza traffic & neon messages?
I take thoughtful journeys to supermarkets,
philosophize about the newest good movie,
camp out at magazine racks & on floors,
catch humanity leering back in laundromats,
invent shortcuts by the quarter hour

There's meaning to all this itemization
& I'd do well to look for it in woodpiles
& in hills & springs & trees in the woods
instead of staying in my shack all the time

thinking too much,
                    falling asleep in old chairs
All those childhood years spent in farmhouses
& I still cant tell one bush from another —
Straight wilderness would wipe me out
faster than cancer from smoking cigarettes

My country friends are out all day long
stomping thru the woods all big-eyed &
that's me walking the road afternoons,
head in some book,
                    all that hilly sweetness wasting

                              Late January
                              Sonoma Mountain Road
                              in the Year of the Dragon

TOPSY: PART 2

How overwhelming
that Lester tune
heard just out of the rain
early one night
in a café bar
full of African students
midtown Madrid
September 1963
young & dumb & lonesome
a long ways from home
amazed at my tall
cheap rum & coke
patting the wetness
from my leathered foot
to that Lester tune
cut by Cozy Cole

blown from a jukebox
right up the street from where
Quixote's Cervantes once died

I ARRIVE IN MADRID

The wretched of the earth
are my brothers.
Neither priest
nor state
nor state of mind
is all God is
who must understand
to have put up for so long
with my drinking & all my restlessness
my hot & cold running around
unwired
to any dogma;
the way I let the eyes
of dark women
in southern countries
rock my head
like a translucent vessel
in turbulent waters.

Long have I longed for adventure,
a peculiar kind of romance
on the high seas of this planet.
Victimized at last
I float alone
exploring time
in search of tenderness,
a love
with no passage attached.

So this is dictatorship,
a watery monday morning
smell of the atlantic
still blowing thru me.
If you have ever died or been born
you will understand
when I speak of everything being salty
like the taste of my mother's tears
when I came back to earth
thru her
after much of the bombing & blood-letting
had taken place here
when Spain was the name of some country
she knew from the words of some popular song
publicized over the radio.

This city too
feels as tho it's held together by publicity
but publicity is going to lose its power
over the lives of men
once we have figured out just what within us
is more powerful & more beautiful
than program or text.

For now
there is language & Spanish to cope with,
there are eyelashes & chromosomes
pesetas pounds francs & dollars
& a poverty even wine cannot shut out.

MALAGUEÑA SALEROSA

for Roberto Mates & for Doris

What beautiful eyes youve got there
underneath your own two eyebrows
underneath your own two eyebrows
what beautiful eyes youve got there

That's Mexican for O youre too much!
I always loved that mariachi song,
learned it on the Three Gold Star Bus
runs out of ratty Tijuana on out
thru dusty Sonora where they stop you
for no reason to search your bags
as if to ask that you promise you wont
do poems about simply what happens,
on up to Michoacán my green Indian dream
to the top of it all — Mexico D.F.

There one night in the big city
Bob & I were happy & fantastic
tripping up Calle Shakespeare,
bourgeois part of town with maids,
arm in arm with joyous Doris
stuck on her NYC politician lover,
Bob brooding his Havana heaven,
me so sad for my only California

We molest a *macho* a jitterbug —
"How far's it from here to Yucatán?"
"Ay hombre as far as I am dronk!"
—only so much kinder in Spanish spoken

Then the four of us arms all linked
danced all the way to quiet Michelet St.
to serenade young Lady D. goodnight

This Mexico City's vanished.
Bob's back in Detroit working welfare.
Doris whoever she was is no more.
There isnt any such jitterbug drunk.
The me of then is gone forever

Good thing the song's still around

JOY/SPRING

Mexico version

All dream, all whim
(not necessarily yours either)
— these fields of Jalisco
the flowery dungsmell

sweet organic smell of
burro & milkcow

A mustache rises into the air
where it's morning always,

widows crunching on popsicle
pat fat tortilla balls.

A man is wobbling
up the road
half drunk with presence
& knowing for sure

some peace that's a preview
of what's waiting for us all.

"Wait your turn!"
his happy eyes sing.

"Wait your turn!"
the tortilla women pat.

Joy gives him reason
to smile in this season

& it's all dream,
dreamers

PONCE DE LEÓN/A MORNING WALK

You too if you work hard enough
can end up being the name of a street
in a drowsy little Indian town
a day's drive from Mexico City
where orphans like bold Joselito
hustle in the taxi burro streets,
where cosmetic fragrances mingle
with scents of ripe & overripe fruits
& vegetables, where the smell of breakfast
& dinner are almost the same.

The natural odor of dung & bodysweat
rises from the zócalo into a sky, semi-
industrialized, housing the spirits of
blue señoritas with sun soaking into
their rain-washed skirts dried dustier
& wrinklier than red or green pepper.

While a crazy rooster's crowing late
a brown baby delights in orange & yellow
balloons floating up like laughter

to tenement windows where a whole family
of older kids wave happy soap wands
that yield fat bubbles part air part
water part light that pop in the faces
of prickly straw behatted gents
rambling by below, ragged & alive —

One morning's moment in this ageless
stone thoroughfare named after just one
dead Spaniard who wanted to live forever

MOON WATCHING BY LAKE CHAPALA

> *I love to cross a river in very*
> *bright moonlight and see the*
> *trampled water fly up in chips*
> *of crystal under the oxen's feet.*
> The Pillow Book of Sei Shōnagon,
> 10th Century

IT CAN BE beautiful this sitting by oneself all alone except for
the world, the very world a literal extension of living leaf, sur-
face & wave of light: the moon for example. American poet
Hazel Hall felt,

> "I am less myself
> & more of the sun,"

which I think upon these
cool common nights being at some remove, in spirit at least,
from where they are busy building bombs & preparing concen-
tration camps to put my people into; I am still free to be in love
with dust & limbs (vegetable & human) & with lights in the
skies of high spring.

IN THE AFTERNOON you watch fishermen & fisherboys in
mended boats dragging their dark nets thru the waters. You can

even buy a little packet of dried sardines like I do, a soda, & lean against the rock & iron railings but you wont be able to imagine the wanderings of my own mustachio'd dad who was a fisherman in Mississippi in the warm streams of the Gulf of Mexico. How time loops & loops! Already I'm drunk with the thought of distances. I do that look skyward & re-chart the con- stellations. No one to drop in on. No one to drop in on me. It's been a long time since I've had nothing better to do than estab- lish myself in one spot & stare directly into the faces of the moon, the golden orange white brown blue moon, & listen to the tock of my heart slowing down in the silence. I can almost hear in the breeze & picture in the sniffable award-winning moonlight the doings & dyings of my hard-working father, of all my heartbroken mamas & dads.

WHO WILL LIVE to write The Role of Moonlight in the Evo- lution of Consciousness?

IN NEW YORK, San Francisco & points in between the sad young men & women are packaging their wounds & hawking them; braggadocios cleansing old blood from syringes & sly nee- dles in preparation for fresh offerings of cold hard chemical bliss: ofays wasted on suburban plenitude; not-together Bloods strung out on dreams.

I'M OUT HERE alone, off to one side, in the soft dark inspect- ing a stripe of tree shadow on my moonlit hand, dissolving into mineral light, quivering donkey light, the waters churning with fish & flora, happiness circulating thru my nervous system like island galaxies thru space.

▼ ▼ ▼

MEXICO CAN BE Moon can be Madness can be Maya. But the rising notion that we are in the process of evolving from ape to angel under the influence of star-gazing is the Dream.

DEAR OLD STOCKHOLM

Of course it is snowing
but two city girls,
one blonde the other black-
haired, are preparing for bed
in a warm apartment they share.
One is washing her hair in the bathroom sink
while the other does hatha yoga exercises.
They have been dancing with some young men
who spoke nothing but north american english,
one of them from Pittsburgh
(from Crawford's Grill up on the Hill)
& the other
a fingerpopper from Leamington, Ontario.

Suddenly, recalling the evening,
the rushing from taxis up inside music clubs,
all of them pleased that it should be so,
the bathroom blonde
who,
like a great many scandinavians,
played some instrument in secondary school
whistles John Coltrane's whole solo
from the Miles Davis *Dear Old Stockholm*
which had been an old swedish folk song.
In fluorescent abandon
& in time
she massages her foamy scalp
with delight.

The young black-haired woman,
hearing all this
—tensed in a shoulderstand,
head full of new blood,
filling with new breath —
is overcome with unexpected happiness.

Each girl smiles in private
at the joyfulness of the evening
& at the music & the men, wishing
it would never end

EVERYWHERE

The apples are still as sweet
as the loquats are plentiful
& the breeze thru both trees
sings promises to me
that the sky reinforces

Like sailors of old
I too am amply tattoo'd
with pictures from a journey
thru lives the yogis say
I myself quite consciously chose

before returning to this planet
to work out hassles
Ive sometimes evaded evenings
with a tilt of the beercan
or the clicking on of music

Inside my skin I am intact
striving to be sweeter to the taste
than apple or loquat or wind
itself. My goals havent changed.
Mingus once said, "Youve probably

written the some way for a million years."
My heart is more tattoo'd than skin
but the wrinkles you see & white hairs
are designs, records, roadmaps

into a region vaster & deeper than

Marlboro Country, an orchard
where harvest isnt always sweet,
a funnytime land of suns & moons
whose only citizen gets lost enough
to signal irreverently for help

CONTINUING

for Jim & Jeanie Houston

Take time as lubricant or
time as deterrent, it can
either oil my gears or stop
me right here in my tracks for
snow or grass to cover up.

Green leaves, red leaves, fallen leaves
— a matter of time, distance,
room for change to happen in.
Death's as much a happening
as birth, a process, a move,
a moving forth always, the
end never in sight except
perhaps to the gifted blind.

How much distance does the heart
cover in one lifetime of
beating? How much love is killed
in its final wising up
to the sad ways of the world?

If Ive ignored time for months
in order to concentrate

on getting by & basics,
it's because a light within
me that once flashed red or green
is gradually yellowing,
casually mellowing me
for lifetimes of vigilance.

DETROIT 1958

Only parts of the pain of living
may be captured in a poem or
tale or song or in the image seen.

Even in life we only halfway feel
the tears of a brother or sister,
mass disenchantment in cities,
our discovery of love's meagerness,
the slow rise and fall of the sun.

Sadness is the theme of existence;
joy its variations. Pain is only a portion
of sadness, and efforts to escape it
can lead to self-destruction,
one aspect of pain lived imaginatively.

It is in life that we celebrate pain;
It is in art that we imitate it,

Beauty is saddening, or, as the man sings,
"The bitter note makes the song so sweet."

MAYA

*The life I've led keeps me from committing
suicide . . .*

Blaise Cendrars

Songbirds gigging all across California
zipping post slowed-down lenses of the waking eye
dont know this bird
a softer bird
a bird me more than shadows I cast
the moon tonight
as fat as a goose
flashing all thru me
funnybird that zooms
like a feeling
straight up
to escape the heart's net
winging
        winging
              further yet
even beyond tantrums
the world throws
aimed at crippling creatures in flight

Sweet tourists of the soul
there never flew a cockatoo
there never was a tiger cub
there never was an antelope
that leaped or dove
more longingly than I
for love
up into that clean white sky
of the eye's mind

There never lived an Asian brother
or Bantu lover
or Cherokee
whose love of floating surpassed my own

Merciful Kali
Bringer & Taker-Away of feathers & bricks
bring me to the true & lasting route to joyfulness
that I may forsake
the use of filthy drugs
not misuse this gift of speech

IDENTITIES

So youre playing
Macbeth in Singapore
1937 before you were
even born perhaps

The lady is warm,
your lines are waiting
in your stomach
to be heard.

An old seacoast drunk
in pullover blue cap
stomps up one-legged
onto the stage to
tell you youve got no
business playing this
bloody Macbeth,
not a lonely black boy
like you, lost like
himself in a new world
where it's no longer
a matter of whom
thou knowest so much
as it is who you know.

(Say the lady warming
is a career bohemian
with OK looks & a
Vassar education)

Say the future seems
fractured in view of
the worsening wars
in Europe & Asia &
the old man's just
shattered your last
chance illusion.

Well, do you go on
& Shakespeare anyway
or reach for the sky
for the 500th time?

2 A.M.

for Arlin J.

My beautiful wife
of the flower nights,
as we sail together
the dawns of consciousness
into days of the sun
from warmed over moons
of our darknesses,

keep in starry memory
how heaven has loaned us
one to the other
long enough only
that each might surrender

nothing that was not once
everything to either
in the lazy waste
of self-indulgence

(& just what could we share
that wouldnt just serve
to reward one's self
or no one?).

Merging like months
to form these years,
light that once blinded
now dazzles us.

You so clearly serve me
in all that you give
that I am ashamed
when I only flash back
thru clouds
my emerging love.

SQUIRRELS

Squirrels are skittering
outside thru the trees
of my bedroom window,
laying it on the line
of my consciousness

Brown & black, furry &
scurrying, how can I not
help loving them like
an old bopster loves licks

laid down building up
so many beats to the moment?

Squirrels may be crazy
but they arent dullards
They like to play too
They cant be hustling nuts &
hoard all the time. Like
everybody else they love
a good chase now & again
Swishing thru branch leaves,
drumming on my diamond roof,
the shining young squirrels
are making & saving the day

THERE IS A SADNESS

for Peter Beagle

There is a sadness to this world

There is a grimness
a nastiness in the throat
a foulness of breath
a slackening of the penis into sorrow
a chill in the bloodstream that hurts
— limitations of fleshhood!
    pain of becoming!
In a spasm of forgetfulness
the seed is sown

There is a ragged edge of my life
a shabby contour
rounding down into nowhere,
the rainyness of wanting

I might well have known
wrestling by the woodstove
in Red Clay Mississippi

There is a tumbling
from noplace to noplace
& there is a crumbling
from nothing to zero,
a journey from germ to germ again
in which the soul travels nowhere
There is such thing as soul,
I have felt it & can feel it moving
within myself & others
in spite of ourselves,
the stolen landscapes we frequent,
the caverns of doubt in which we hide

There is such thing as life &
it is not this bleak intermission
during which I scurry for bread & lodging
or judge myself by my failures

O there is a shadowy side of my house
where old dreams harbor
where longings go up in smoke
where a cold & ugly opposite of love
is burning under the sun

TRIBUTE

Yes brothers you invented jazz
& now I'm inventing myself
as lean & prone to deviance
as the brilliance of your
musical utterance, a wind
that sweeps again & again
thru my American window
What a life you sent me
running out into expecting
everyone to know at once
just what it was I was
talking or not talking about

The genius of our race
has far from run its course
& if the rhythms & melody
I lay down this long street
to paradise arent concrete
enough it can only be because
lately Ive grown used to taking
a cozier route than that of
my contemporary ancestors

Where you once walked or ran
or railroaded your way thru
I now fly, caressing the sturdy
air with balls of my feet
flapping my arms & zeroing

FOR POETS

Stay beautiful
but dont stay down underground too long
Dont turn into a mole
or a worm
or a root
or a stone

Come on out into the sunlight
Breathe in trees
Knock out mountains
Commune with snakes
& be the very hero of birds

Dont forget to poke your head up
& blink
Think
Walk all around
Swim upstream

Dont forget to fly

THE MOVE CONTINUING

All beginnings start right here.
The suns & moons of our spirit
keep touching.
I look out the window at rain
& listen casually to latest developments
of the apocalypse
over the radio
barely unpacked &
hear you shuttling in the backgrounds
from one end of the new apartment
to the other

bumping into boxes of personal belongings
I cant remember having touched 48 hours ago.
Jazz
a very ancient music
whirls beneficently
into our rented front room.

I grow back thru years
to come upon myself
shivering
in my own presence of long ago
when the bittersweet world
passed before
(rather than thru)
me

a vibrant collage
of delights
in supercolor.

It wasnt difficult becoming a gypsy,
At one end of the line
there was God.
& at the very other end
there is God.
In between
shine all the stars of all the spaces
illuminating everything
from the two tender points
that are your eyes
to the musical instruments
of these strong but gentle black men
glowing on the LP in the dark,
the darkness of my own heart
beating its way along
thru all the evenings
that lengthen my skies,
all the stockings
that have ever been rolled down

sadly,
lover & beloved
reaching
to touch one another
at this different time
in this different place
as tho tonight were only the beginning
of all those
yester-
days

Geography of the Near Past
(1976)

BACKTRACKING

for Arl

Ive already told you about the dance,
the wayward song, the way the moon
follows me up into bed on the chance
something might come tumbling down soon.

Well, whatll it be this time around,
what kind of silence or tight blue light
is there to be broken, gathered, or found
as winter freezes over our shoulders tonight?

The only pictures we've ever lent you,
whisper our windows being looked out of,
are of sunshine & snow you keep walking into
as you would a mirror, an eyeful of love.

What say this time I pick up your lead
& follow you back to the only real need?

ELEGY

Ted Cunningham (1926–1971)

Good morning!
Good morning!
Good morning!

This was your greeting
all day long.

Walking into your home
the first thing one noticed
was always music.

Walking into your life
the first thing one felt
was always music.

How could a man like you
not sing, not play, not dance,
not stretch mornings
into midnight?

When you gave yourself
in true matrimony
to one beautiful woman
you both made *Jet* magazine:
Black Ex-Priest Weds Ex-Nun
or words to that effect.

The real story would make
anyone's heart pound
with admiration & affirm
the sacredness of being alive.

Neither the Church
nor the Jesuit order
was expansive enough
or windowless enough
to contain the breadth
of your spirit.

You were blessed with only
one child of your own & yet
countless children must have
cherished your fatherly touch.

Good morning —
it isnt enough to simply
preach about loving the poor.

Good morning —
there's so much work to be done!

Good morning —
there's no time to waste!

"Good morning!" you sang
for the next-to-last time
to your remarkable wife
to your six-month-old daughter
to the grandmother who raised you
to all of your friends
remembered, recorded, live.

Good morning, Omaha!
Good morning, Nairobi!
Good morning, New York!
Good morning, Vatican City!
Good morning, California!
Good morning, bureaucracy!
Good morning, cancer!
Good morning, suffering!
Good morning, brothers & sisters!

Along with everything else
you taught that elegies &
memorial rituals were for
the living to console the living.
If yesterday or tomorrow
meant anything to you
you quietly never showed it.

You didnt practice selflessness,
you had it down pat & lived it
in one bright, endless morning.

This world that you moved thru
but were not attached to
is, perhaps without knowing it,
all the lonelier for your absence,
all the richer for your presence.

"Good morning!" you said.

Good morning, Ted.

FOR ARL IN HER SIXTH MONTH

Cool beneath melon-colored cloth, your belly —
a joyous ripening that happens & happens,
that gently takes root & takes over,
a miracle uncelebrated under an autumn dress
that curves & falls slowly to your ankles.

As you busy yourself with backyard gardening,
humming, contained, I think of your tongue
at peace in its place; another kind of fruit,
mysterious flower behind two lips that open
for air & for exits & entrances.

                              Perhaps if I placed
my hungry ear up next to a cantaloupe or coconut
(for hours at a time & often enough),
I'd hear a fluttering or maybe a music almost like
the story Ive heard with my ear to your belly,
a seashell history of evolution personified.

Your womb is a room where it's always afternoon.

STUDIO UP OVER IN YOUR EAR

The radiator's hissing hot
My Smith-Corona's cleaned & oiled
with a fresh nylon ribbon
for the hard miles ahead

Gurney Norman's notes for his book
scribbled against this flaking wall
painted landlord green grow more
cryptic as the nights wear on
This used to be his working place

The sky over University Avenue
from my second-story window is
clean, calm, & black again in this
sudden warm night in December

Sleepily my inner voice thins
as, entering my characters' worlds,
I see all of life as unedited film
with no title, no lion, no Paramount
spangle of stars to soften what's ended,
altho everybody gets in on the credits

Far away, in the cabaret downstairs,
Asleep at the Wheel (a western country band)
breaks em up as their loud lead singer,
a little brunette with Woolworth's
in her voice, belts out, "You wanna
                    take me for a ride in the
                    backseat of your cawrr!"

Out on the sidewalk just below my half-
opened window three young men split
a fifth of Bali Hai & shoot the shit
& some craps 1940s-style to the music

Up here in freelance heaven

Ive got my own floating game going on

The ante is tremendous & side bets
are OK, but youre lucky if you walk out
with the clothes on your back

> December 26, 1972
> Palo Alto, California
> *Written three nights before the*
> *cabaret In Your Ear burned down*

THE NIGHT BEFORE MICHAEL WAS BORN

The picture is simply chile relleno,
chicken enchilada, refried beans &
rice with lettuce salad, cold beer

by the plainest doorway, cropping out
a vanishing world we never fit into
nor of which we've ever been fans.

It's warm in here but cold outside.
Our nervous feet touch under the table.
Can the baby inside you take hot sauce?

NOT HER, SHE AINT NO GYPSY

Fifteen years up & her tongue's still flapping
She lives in the calcium of her bones
She lives in the toughness of her liver
She lives in the memory of men she's made happy by surprise
That's her salvation for now, for the weekend

She raised a son this way but she wont get to heaven
Her heaven's got jukeboxes anyway
Lots of jukeboxes & well-peppered shot glasses, a little bush
    on the side, coin telephones
Her son's a nice kid, digs cars & girls & unh-hunh the North
    Pole, collects books & articles on it & secretly hopes to visit it
Just another almost American boy with a mixed-up sisterly mom

She was beautiful once, a wild way-out kid (as they said in
    those days) who'd try anything once, twice if it was nice enough
She's still beautiful in another kind of way
But she dont know this just yet
All she know is she still got ice & a lotta drink left & the
    happy-headed dude across the table say he just sold a tune
    to some rock band & they threw in a little coke to boot so
    drink up love there's plenny more where this is coming
    from baby

She gets high to connect with ecstasy & pretty soon before she
    know it everything gets to be all elemental
Even as she pulls her panties up & kisses old hairy what's-
    his-name good morning she still dont know just what it is
    that's been bugging her all this time & how come her boy
    turned out so straight

But that's how it go
That's just how it go
She wouldnt change now, she couldnt come down for all the
    pills in Beverly Hills, for all the booze in Veracruz

She aint sold out yet & her tongue's still flapping

THE SAD HOUR OF YOUR PEACE

Elevator music from a Tokyo radio
leaks out slowly across the sand,
across greased backs, along oiled bellies
blackening in sunlight, browning, reddening

Squeezed in now, beach almost within reach,
there's no leaving right away, no casual getaway
You drove forty miles to arrive at this truce

Now there's only warm beer for refreshment
& leftover dreams to swim around & drown in
to the rise & fall of your own hot stomach
as the world breathes you in & out again

Out beyond your basic toes — the ocean,
sloshing & flashing like a liquid flame

Youre flat on your back again, goofy tunes
evaporating at your earlobes; ball-chasing
kids stomp tiptoe across your ribs
The fading glow of people you dont know
hogs up the sky & bright distances

Youre dreaming of a beach you walked alone
as a kid in a movie that was never even shot

                                        Santa Cruz

REDISCOVERED DIARY ENTRY

A glass of sweet milk
(stirred with honey)
warm by my cold Underwood
There's a woman asleep in my bed

Today I gorged myself on ice cream
& said several prayers
for energy to continue

Today I shook hands formally with
an old robed Zen master from Japan
whose head glistened youthfully
like the skin of a new golden apple
rubbed lovingly against a sleeve

Too many Aprils ago we
boarded the same bus mornings
in Berkeley with its plum blossoms
I would be on my way to work
He would simply be on his way
Today our fresh paths touched

Breathing before the pale wall of
my tiny writing room tonight,
I dissolve into all of the magazine
cutouts Ive carefully put up
to remind myself how lonely I am

Sleep must wait until daylight now
when the lady will leave for work
& I will already have done mine
Tonight in silence I sip my milk &
salute the snoring of the radiator

Today I am on my way

A MORNING POEM FOR MICHAEL

Where in the new fruit
lies its sweet color?
And how dare we say that
death is taking place
with such & such a being
when all the time an
ageless delight is setting in
that pleases even a
tender two-year-old?

Could it be there in
the mystery & joy we seek
& feel in connecting with.
the soft flesh of others?

VISITING DAY

for Conyus

This being a minimum security facility, it feels more like being
on a reservation than in a touchable cage

Books are allowed, smiles, eats (you could slip a .38 inside a
baked chicken or a file inside a loaf of sourdough french
easily enough, but there's really not much to shoot or saw
thru)

You sign up, take a seat at one of the open-air picnic tables, &
yawn from hours of driving into the beautiful chilled
morning

All the black inmates trudging by or hanging out of barracks
   windows give you the power salute as you consider yourself
   again strapped down in their skins
You walk, you talk, you toy around with words, you steal
   guarded looks down into one another

A little food, fruit juice, a lot of gossip, & the sun on the trees
   under blue sky surrounding us is magnified into one big
   silly-looking halo

"I'm not into meat all that much anymore, man, & there's a
   whole lotsa books I wanna talk about & — here, these're
   some things I wrote last month — thinking about that last
   letter I wrote you where I said my head was getting peace-
   ful — what's the bloods on the block woofing about these
   days?"

He looks healthier than he did in the old macrobiotic city yogi
   wild bustling days when you'd both get zonked on sounds
   in the middle of the aftenoon & reminisce for midnights
   about stuff that probably never happened

This is what's known as a conservation camp where you cut &
   prune trees, dig up the earth, seed the ground, weather
   watch, sweat a lot, do a little basketball, sun on the run,
   sneak peeks at crotch shots in magazines smuggled in from
   outside

You think of his woman, you think of his son, you think of
   them holed up alone in the city, waiting & waiting for him
   to come home

You think of all the professionals involved: pipe smokers with
   advanced degrees from state colleges — penologists, crimi-
   nologists, sociologists who minored in deviate psychology;
   in clean, classy ghettos where they never take walks, their
   children snort coke on an allowance

Three tables away from where you sit consoling one another,
  a slim young man up on a burglary rap is splitting his
  attention between a 2-year-old daughter & a 22-year-old
  wife who's shown up thoughtfully in tight-fitted jeans
  ripped generously enough to allow him to see what she
  hasn't bothered wearing

Well, it isnt San Quentin, it isnt Attica, & it's no one's official
  prisoner of war camp, yet you cant help thinking there's
  a battle going on somewhere out there in the bloodstreams
  of men

You say good-bye, you shake hands good-bye, you stare good-
  bye; you wave what you havent said, you grin what you
  cannot say, you walk away & turn again to wave what
  neither of you has to say

You gun your engine good-bye & roar off down the California
  road back out into your own special prison

Weeks later you hear about the steel file some white inmate's
  driven into the heart of another white inmate found by your
  friend by some bushes in the rain — dead — because he was
  your friend's good friend, because he was a nigger lover, a
  nigger lover

The news chills the tips of your fingers & you sweat

Could it have been the father of the sweet little girl, husband
  of the gal whose ass was showing?

Could it have been the marijuana dealer who read the *Bhaga-
  vad Gita* & meditated nightly?

Could it have been the small-boned cat thief who spoke
  Spanish with an Italian lilt like an Argentinian?

Could it have been the crinkly eyed loser who made you laugh
    & laugh when he talked about his life inside & outside the
    joint like a stand-up comic?

You think about the first person you ever screamed at

You think about the first thing you ever stole, or lied about,
    or killed

HERRICK HOSPITAL, FIFTH FLOOR

*for a musician friend who
finally OD'd on Blackness*

Well, so youve gone & overdone it again,
overdosed yourself this time on Blackness;
locked between Blue Cross, nurse-padded walls,
the unreliable air outside & beyond
shot up with softening Berkeley sunshine

Phrasing fails you, diction cramps,
words are a loss & reflection too costly
What color were you ever but infamous blue?

If your music werent sound & its realness
didnt cleanse, I know you could never walk
much less dance out of this white room again

GREEN IS A FEELING, NOT A COLOR

In the branches of your nerves
a draft passes, as in sleep
in a storm, as the tree bends
in nights no Columbus could sail

In summer an apple shines hollow
with many suns inside it, dreaming
women swimming slowly sandy shores
in green & yellow, bikinis that smile

There's nothing new here, just
an ancient new world: a picture of
stones & flesh slipping into an ocean
into chilled kisses, caresses, as a
child would a boot or carousel spinning
with flashing pink tongues, warm teeth

Leaves of your body are flying away,
original birds, flat without mouths,
out to backyards away from the sea
across dream sand the color of burnt snow

In the branches of your nerves
leaves must only be extensions of
all our trembling treeflesh, starflesh,
the body with arms held out, a star,
five-pointed, perfect to hang space
around or light for leaf or galaxy

Love, I feel you leafless, a field
the greenness of my own invention

MOSS

The Rolling Stones,
a hard English group,
busted for heroin
at their Southern France estate,
fifty grams of smack a week
said the man on the news
just to keep
their little family extended

Well, so what,
whatll happen to them?
So what if the air
back of these superstars
gets waved away
from time to time
like those costly backdrops
in the old film factories?

Charles Christopher Parker,
a genius among geniuses,
was granted diplomatic immunity
the moment that he died

Eleanora Fagan Gough
(the Billie Holiday who now
powers many a Silver Cloud)
was a sufferer among sufferers
with narks up in her deathbed

Even Bela Lugosi,
our beloved Transylvanian,
sustained his habit in real life
& metaphorically on screen

Ah the Rolling Stones,
a hard English group,
heroes of an American era

DEMEROL

The glamour of this moment too will pass.
This bright warm wind that whispers thru me now,
thru my body, a dwelling place of spirit,
will blow itself away.

               Like laughing gas
that dentists used in 1910 for pain,
this sweet drug even now feels out-of-date.
Is it their muzak oozing from the walls,
crisp leaves of city trees quivering with rain
outside this clinic window where I lie
that make me sad & at the same time feel
that I could swim this sinking stream of joy
forever? — no how-are-you, no good-bye.

Delicious as it seems, it doesnt last.
Having to do it over & over again
means keeping up with Joneses that dont die.

AMERICAN GLAMOUR

Is my dress appropriate?
Is my breath still fresh?
Will my underarms fail me?
What about my hair?
Should I have gotten it shaped,
is it long enough
to proclaim to one & all
my true & lasting blackness?

It's the 7 A.M. flight.
Even the plane seems to yawn
as they test its engines

one by one in the historic fog of
San Francisco International.

The stewardesses in their
miniskirted uniforms,
designed by some promotional committee
to make them look pretty & sexy,
look silly, look shot, look
O so American cheesecake!

There arent enough minutes
between now & landing to
savor these ridiculous niceties:
coffee in flight, token sweet roll,
documentary voice of the pilot
droning the time, temperatures,
                altitudes, cruising speeds . . .

Dozing amid commuters who'd fall
into deep sleep if they only knew
they were up here with a poet
trying to play his nuttiness down,
I'm on my way to interview
the great Ray Charles on assignment.

Pacific Southwest Airlines into L.A. today
— tomorrow? Who knows? Trans World!

ROLAND NAVARRO (1939–1961)

I leave you on that downtown street of
how many Detroit winters ago, standing
in front of the March of Dimes display
in a window, wincing aloud to me of suffering
people all over the world where a boy
cut out of cardboard on crutches implores,
"Please won't you help? Please won't you give?"

You were home from West Point, the holidays,
still owing me a big bottle of vodka from
some high-school bet that's as dark & forgotten
as any old joke from the shadowy past.

You wanted to be a big general down in
South America, Argentina, where your skilled dad
took refuge after twenty years of visiting you
weekends at his parents' home, your grand-
parents' house on Clairmount not far from
12th Street where we each caught buses, sometimes
together, & lived straight out of our heads
littered with print, pictures, & old pianos —
you Chicano, me black, both of us niggers.

We loved the same girls more than once &
you wrote in a letter how I should think twice
about becoming a poet or artist of any kind
because the mad world had no more need of
that kind of craziness: *"They grind you down
and fuck you around, then toss you a crumb or
a well-gnawed bone, then shit on you again."*
You told me, *"Be a soldier, be an ass kicker,
& get in on the take by starting at the top."*

How many times we played your Napoleon game
with paper ships & troops in war-torn Novembers!
Cursing like a sailor, upsetting my mother,

you wrote enough of an epic novel to impress
the hell out of me along with your drawings
& that piano piece of yours called *Funeral Bells*.
I still have the portrait you did of me when
I was studying trumpet — *Young Horn with a Boy*.

So your father remarried, a woman more our age,
leaving you with snapshots of your mother,
a legend who died before you'd learned to love.
I leave you watery-eyed in front of that paper
publicity cripple, you who wanted to rule men
tall in your shiny black Argentine boots,
frightened by a tenderness your heart couldnt rule.
Here the world ends, here the sun's hidden
forever from a scene you abandoned slyly
to return to your bright new Connecticut love
whose photo you flashed reminded me of
your lost mamá & a princess named Juanita
(uncrowned object of our junior-high search)
but this sure-enough Her Highness was rich
& fair.
             Come that summer you'd finally marry
the goddess you always accused me of seeking.

You did it, you did it, you outfoxed fate!
You survived the honor system & graduated clean.
I looked forward to studying you in histories
to come but the world & impatience got in the way.
All that Pérez Prado we'd been thru together,
all that Mingus, Debussy, *Swan Lake* & the Penguins,
Rimbaud, Charlie Parker, Tolstoi, Cézanne, Joe Loco
wasnt enough to head off an ending I'd rather
imagine than know as I did Vivian or Nina,
as I know the moon of honey Mexico where you died
in an auto crash that killed you outright &
left your bride crippled like that poster child.

I think of you always, I even hum your song
here where what's right must collide with what's wrong.

1961–1973

HO

She coulda been somethin
like the Supremes or somebody
Her folks give her everything she need
I use to know her family pretty good
They dont have that much but they
     aint on relief
She call herself in love

Her money it go for that stuff, I guess,
    & for strong mouthwash, I know
I see her buyin Baby Ruths & Twinkies too
    down at the liquor store

Every night she start her day
right under my window when the lights
    come on
She aint bad-lookin neither, just little

She just a skinny little sister
bout big as my fist
but even she done slipped & found out
heaven aint the only H in the dictionary

MAKING LOVE AFTER HOURS

Back up in the room they snap on
all-nite movies but leave the sound
turned down, turned off.
                              You see,
neon & smoke last just so long & soon
there're no more joints to haunt
or get lost in, no more ghosts to give up
except the flicker & ripple of TV light
against their shot bodies quivering with shadow.

With an urgency of children permitted to
stay up way past bedtime, they share,
they linger, they nurse the last drink.
They whisper & they whisper, sighing to collapse.

She peels off her turtleneck,
undoes her jeans, kicks her sandals
straight toward the window as the moon comes up
shining thru clouds in a rainy 1930s
tight-suit movie, too mellow a moon,
like some yawning display in a budget-store window.

For week & weeks he's dragged around feeling
sorry for himself but now unalone, naked
next to her, he just cant remember how much
        or how come.

Two stories down, drunks stumble the streets
in search of some phone booths to pee in.

REALISM

Socialist Realism & Capitalist Realism
are the same thing

I am thinking this way &
walking down Shattuck with my wife
when I catch the sign in
Woolworth's window

Lifelike
PLASTIC
FLOWERS
with
built-in-bloom
washable
nonallergic
prices
as marked
Satisfaction Guaranteed
or
money refunded

So knowing a good poem
when I see one I copy it down
on the back of the brown envelope
from the Telephone Company that says —
EXTENSION PHONES take the run
out of RUNNING A HOME!

HEAD OF A WOMAN

That gypsy strain is
daubed into her eyes

the hair brushed on
so blackly with care

brown face brown neck
round jaw wide face

smooth stylized ear
with airy ring of cloud

at its lobe for decor.
Her mouth is that full

human-lipped love mouth
ripe & sensuous, as they say

in poems, but which painters
show. The green shawl

she's been wearing slips
down to delight us with

a bundle of shoulder also
brown, brown the color

brown the evening air
framed ever so softly

in breathable surroundings
of imaginary light.

MANHATTAN MARCH, THE 1970s

A black teenager strapped to
the baby boy on her back
straight out the South or some
unnoticed Connecticut slum
crowded with media promise
steps up to ask me one midnight
if I know a hotel nearby in
the neighborhood where they can
put up for the night reasonable

How bout the Chelsea?
Tried it but they want too much!

Too much is involved
Too much anger
Too much softness

Her lovely hard eyes
look way down into me

I know the no-man's-land
she's running away from by now

Stop some driver &
ask the taxi, I say,
which she does cautiously
over my skyscraped shoulder

The world is you
The world is me

The world is you with
me strapped to its back

FUN CITY SAMBA

for Ann McIntosh

Even being able to get a glimpse of moon
in a sky tacked up over West 22nd Street
that I didnt know existed in New York
is motive enough for celebration

What do I do next, is it proper to smile?
Is it bad city form to whistle & jangle
gently as you walk (like Satchel Paige says)
to keep the juices flowing, to avoid running
at all times?

       Ive almost never looked back
on myself in this city designed so much
for the moment that even the pain of peeking
out the window at 2 A.M. to check out a
modishly pantsuited, fortyish woman swearing
& crying, bumping into parked cars,
screaming up at the window of a lover
she almost got together with in the bar
around the corner is only instant Off-B'way

EAST BOSTON

for Denise Levertov

Up in this warm, solid house of yours
while you make breakfast I stand sighing
at the window, breaths away from
this working-class block where trash cans
lined up in front of old buildings
look natural with sun shining down on them

If my heart seems to leap from my shirt
away away away from this instant it's
because the short drive in from Logan Airport
thru last night's minute of neighborhood
streetlight with children playing in it
is whisking me back thru my decades again

Way past dark we chased one another
We had our own style of stickball too
when the England you smiled in wasnt so new

If my voice is quivering it's also because
the sky up over your Boston Inner Harbor
is too splendid to look at this morning —
cool waters below, those barges so sober!

Ive lived for so long now on another coast

PROVIDENCE, RHODE ISLAND

It's spring again
the early part when
the wettest wind
gives you a licking
youll never forget

You stand quivering
down by the Biltmore
whistling for taxis
as maxiskirted women
flee the scene
youve just stepped into

The grayness of this
white water city feels

good to blood that wants
to explode on century's notice
shattering calendar meat
& appointments well kept

Colonial afternoons
had to be colder than
the hearts of witches
laid to rest beneath
these charming city paved hills

Rushing for cover
you now understand the
cooled-out literalness
of these old wooden homes

A skinny black man
(a brother you guess)
who commutes between
this stop & Harlem U.S.A.
tells you he's never been to
Brown or the School of Design
but he know for a fact that
it's Mafia keep this town relaxed

"They got the highest houses
up in them hills but after them
come all your professors & pro-
fessionals, people with a
high-class license to steal"

You want to come back in
summer when the change takes
place but this brilliant chill
has tightened your head

New England is a poker game too

NEW ORLEANS INTERMISSION

A lighted window holds me like
high voltage. I see . . .
Walter Benton,
This Is My Beloved

1

I see it zooming down
over the bayou late April
morning of the brightest green
from the window of a jet named Nancy

Settling back childishly
in the sky all alone,
my secret hand waves light aside
to get a better look at
all the music coiling up
inside me again as I watch
this still virgin landscape

Is that the famous Mississippi
down there, are those the streets
Jelly Roll did his marching,
strutting, & poolsharking in?
Was I really just born
a gulf away from here or
carved like Pinocchio
from some thick dark tree below?

2

The only way to love a city's
to live in it till you know
every door every store every
parkingmeter deadlawn alleycat
district smell pussy hotel
gumwrapper & wino by heart

Airborne all night my sleepy heart
leaps like windblown raindrops

I'm a very old baby reentering
an unchanged world with a yawn

    3

Yes Ive lived here before
just as I know & can feel in my tongue
that Ive tramped this earth as
storyteller & unaccountable thief
too many times before,
a displaced lover of spirit & flesh

Riding the St. Charles trolley nights
an old American, classically black,
spots me as a tourist & softly explains
how he dont have to take snapshots
no more since he can more or less
picture in his mind what's keepable

When I take this 15¢ ride, the cool
off-hour breeze tightening my skin,
I can tune in to people telling their
stories real slow in the form of asides
& catch myself doing a lot of smiling
to hold back tears

                     Old-timer tells me
why the fare on this line's so cheap:
"It's so the colored maids & cooks &
gardeners can git to they jobs & back
without it bein a strain on they pocket"

    4

On Bourbon Street (North Beach or
Times Square) a fan-tailed redhead in

G-string & nothing else waves me
into a topless/bottomless joint with a
dog-faced barker posted at the door
who yips & howls: "C'mon in yall & see
southron gals takin off they draws
for just the price of a drink!"

                              It isnt
enough to laugh & rush in like a
prospective drunk in heat

The point is that love & love alone
holds up my feet as they step from
Bourbon to Rampart Street, dreaming of
Congo Square, Creole intrigue, Fats
Domino & Dr John while a black panhandler
(cross between Satchmo & Papa John Creach)
hits on me for 50¢ in front of Al Hirt's

        5

Steaming hot down in front of us now:
ham biscuit eggs grits Cajun coffee
& a solid glass of buttermilk for me
for fun —

            It's Mama's in the morning
where American poet Miller Williams
leans past his dark wife, Jordan, to say:
"You probly the only Californian that
really knows about this place, man"

I know I'll slip back by for gumbo,
for lunch known down here as dinner,
or for a supper of 90¢ crawfish bisque

But right now it's the light quivering
in from the street down onto our plates
that makes us quit talking poetry

"I'd give up writing," Miller sighs,
"if I could sing as good as Ray Charles"

Tomorrow theyll drive back to the Ozarks
Tomorrow I'll fly back to California
where there're no nickel phone calls,
pick up the show from where I left off
& read Marie Laveau the Voodoo Queen

CITY HOME DETROIT

Old emotions like powdery tenements
undulate in the July heat.
It would take an ocean of sentiment
to cool your memories of this street
that first contained your notions of how
the world operates, how it is what it is.

How your body sweats & pours now
as it prepares to deal with the quiz
that's been haunting you all these years
of walking the earth, stepping thru time,
refining your eyesight, opening your ears
for a liberating music, scales you can climb.

What if you never had run from this race
(Cleveland to Detroit to Chicago, New York)?
What if you'd settled & stayed in your place
among friends who'd never arrive at that fork
in the road of their flat midwestern lives
where Atlantic & Pacific equals A & P,

where rock salt's for winter, & when summer arrives
wish for showers to ease the humidity?

In your California sandals & flowery shirt,
hair a juicy network of coils & strands,
hoping today you won't get robbed or hurt,
you know what forced you to seek other lands.

DUDE IN DENVER

This skinny little dude
up next to a mountain
(the Rockies, eastern slope)
with his wimp mouth look,
cap not even fitting
his pointed head right

His lips hang out from his
mouth & kinda to one side
so when he talk they flap
just enough so you can spot him
from grand distances

He takes a sip of 7Up
from a can swiped from a truck,
adjusts the floppy collar of
his leather coat & Big Apple cap,
blinks behind winter shades
as a cold-blooded Lincoln snores by

Skied over, he undergoes a change
of nerve, looking over both shoulders
to make sure no one's watching
before approaching the parked bike
left unlocked by some college-looking

white girl who could show up any
minute to blow the whistle for good
on this good thing he thinks he's got

Oppression? Repression? Suppression?
Depression? The pressure he's under,
were it ever let out, might heat up
this windblown November afternoon

Can he really be as sad as he looks
now, hunched over in need of a ten-speed
bicycle, cheerless, thin, a thief so
leery of anything passing in the light
within reach of his wet, greedy eyes? —

A Colorado colored boy, Afro, American,
a downright American little dude

ANY INNER CITY BLUES

It would be so easy,
afternoons particularly,
to go take that leap
off the Golden Gate
or run full speed head-on
into the legendary path
of anyone's unpaid-for auto
or shoot up a tablespoon of smack
& lie down in the middle of
the James Lick Memorial Freeway

Or to be modern,
contemporary at least —
give your heart to know
folly & false daring:

race thru the ruins of what was
hip once, pollinating flowerchildren
            at large;
small visible recompense for
a hurt that burns to be eradicated,
not multiplied, like
the head-splitting cancer
that surrounds you

MEXICO CITY LOVER

for Matt Kahn

Going back to D.F.
soon as he can
take a pesero
down the Reforma
straight to her
dollar hotel,
bottle of Bacardi
under one arm
& his heart under
the other beating
like the wings
of a fearful chicken
in the arms
of its raiser
on a third-class bus
to the city

While the kids're
grabbing at balloons
in Chapultepec Park
& the chicks're
snapping Chiclets

in rosy-roofed mouths
he'll slip his free arm
around her waist &
jaywalk her to heaven
under the hefty
smog-prevention trees
limb around trunk
trucks whizzing past
while vaudeville horns
jam traffic music

They can more than
work it on out,
the town'll be theirs
the hours their pink zone
shadows & all
the pulse-stopping dawn
an unfillable trophy
of light for some
a toucher of others
as they kiss in the bowels
of a city neither
of them has chosen for
home on this clay ball
in this stone & steel
Tenochtitlán love nest

CALIFORNIA PENINSULA: EL CAMINO REAL

In 15 minutes
the whole scene'll change
as bloated housewives
hems of their skirts greased
with love mouths wide open
come running out of shops

dragging their young
moon in their eyes
the fear upon them

Any minute now
the gas-blue sky over El Camino Real
is going to droop for good
shut with a squish &
close them all in like
a giant irritated eye

Theyll scramble for cars
the nearest road out
clutching their steering wheels
like stalwart monkeys

It couldve happened yesterday
It couldve happened while they
were sighing in Macy's Walgreen's 31 Flavors
Copenhagen Movies or visiting the Colonel
like that earthquake night
that shattered L.A.

Whatll they will their children then?
Whatll they leave for them to detest?
What tree, what lip print, what Jack in
what Box, what ugly hot order to go?

Already I can smell the darkness
creeping in like the familiar shadow
of some beloved fake monster
in a science fiction flick

In 15 minutes
48 hours days weeks months
years from now all of thisll be
a drowsy memory barely tellable
in a land whose novelty was speech

GEOGRAPHY OF THE NEAR PAST

The trick
without anyone's
catching on to it
is to swim against
world current
knowing it to be as much a dream
as it is drama on the highest stage
but without losing touch
with spirit or with light

Realer even
is to move as if
nothing has ever happened
which is likewise
as true as foam or fog

Each universe is only
an ever-shifting sea
in the surfacing eyes of former fish

SOME RECENT FICTION

> *How do we separate fiction from reality?*
> *Medical students recited Galen*
> *to the effect that some particular bone*
> *belonged to the breast at the very moment*
> *it was being extracted from the foot.*
>
> Evan S. Connell,
> *Points For a Compass Rose*

1

He ran his hands thru her hair
slowly
as tho he were relishing the feel
of expensive Italian corduroy.
The light of Venus did a little dance
way over in the eastern sky.
"Spring again,"
she murmured,
moving herself thru water
soft brown breasts bobbing gingerly
sending electric symbols thru him,
for the extent of his naïveté
was a pubic thing
known publicly by his mother.
Zara is running thru fields of poppies,
she scoops five fingers of cool earth
& rubs it into her cheeks
in fierce denial of her albescence,
funky cloud passing over the moon itself.
"Get it on,
you little s'pose-to-be white girl!"
shouts Superspook in a fit of pique.
He knew her other lover,
the very pig who represented
all white savagery to him,
cloaked society
that by dint of respectability could . . .

The Pig can always move in brother
with his heavy weapons
& blow us away
— his ultimate fear revisiting him,
cool young girl trembling
under his hard erotic touch.
"Hell I'll up & make me an anthem of my own!"
the black voice was heard to declare
cutting thru the narcotic haze of memory
that shimmered over the room to the very
stained-glass windows
built on bitter black sweat.
A little thing drifted back from childhood,
he knew at last the meaning of meaning,
thoughts of wilderness
& the touch of what was
& what was not sexual
purely
a little dream victory galloping thru him.
"I love you, Hitler."
She remembered that phrase
spoken in earnest
& established
by white-haired literati
whom she had once esteemed
in her windblown university days
at Bootlick State.

The two men & the girl
at sunrise
writhed quietly
in rock agony
as the radio clock
buzzed & bounced with all the beats.

All skies fizzled.

2

It is the time of the prosaic showdown.
Noon & Dickens brighten her bones.
She knew the time was coming
when she would be required to brandish a gun
& wave it in the face of even best friends,
of poor Agnes the pathetic acid
head
in whose loins
the Afro-Anglo-Indian milieu
revolved like an IBM typewriter ball
splattering piecemeal
her spiralworm tape-code genetics
more complex than thunderbird circuitry
made naked
by degrees.
"If I had my way
I would lick the very white from your eyes
I would
& jet you away up & out of this melting pot
become pressure cooker,"
he pronounced
reminding her of Thad
when they were first wed
in office-worker Cleveland
the 35¢ wedding soup
& his acting their only hope
her city welfare childhood
Pa packing them all up to them opportunity
cities the smoke choking
even the sodas had soot on the surface
& overpsychoanalyzed Frederick
poor chump seeking to seduce
her irate Trinidadian stepmother
before the blue of her world
turned ashen rose
wind cutting thru
her mind

like lust
the baby so far away
the FM loneliness
Scotches & marijuanas Rod would bring.
Thad would wound her if he found out
cold blade of life cutting
her down & opening up her vegetable heart,
the uneaten orders
unheard ballads
undusted shelves
the tinned fruits & soups on shelves,
the jolly green giantess
trembling in the world air
that closes in
like a trap,
like a suburb
Tuesdays.

3

I shot my sweet tongue down into her craw
& pulled the knife from its heart of veins
everything happening & running
together like blood.
Zara, if you love me
kiss this manuscript
take me back thru guillotine days
the women hanging all off me
the gambles I took
to come out straight
a bright-haired
bright-eyed advocate
of everything interesting
interesting & healthy
the healthy films that are going to be made
the big tits
box office
the way they forced me into Confederate uniforms
the perils of Atlantic

guns my ma left me in her will
to shoot down Billy
the time you thrilled me in Rome
& the ravishing beans they kept pushing on me
in New Orleans.
Kiss me with your Quasimodo lips
hug me Raskolnikov
press me to your bosom Che.
If you will soothe me
just a shade more
I will tell you why our president
deserves the medal more than Zeus,
I will tell you
why I love my own consciousness
more than anything
& we can set the puke-
colored flags of
all inferior countries
out to dry
on windowsills of the word
the world enemy
& map some neocolonialist pimp
gentle reader
creep who buys my hustle.
Kiss this revolutionary on the lips,
everybody tingling,
you must esteem me perfectly
in the passes Ive made toward Virtue
& if I flounder ever
it is because everyman
adores himself
in my new city skin.

TEACHING

There's no such thing as a student,
only abiding faces unwilling
to change except with time,
the oldest force that still fools us

So you teach a feeling,
a notion learned the hard way,
a fact, some figures,
a tract, some rigors of childhood

The face out there
interacting with yours
knows how to grin & play with its pen
but misses the point so charmingly

A thousand moves later
that same shiny face
moving thru the world with
its eyes glazed or fully closed
reconnects with one of its own childhoods

Loosely we call this learning

THE NEW MYSTIC

The waters I'm going to go walking beside,
vibrations Ive been taking into my system,
the cool nourishing breeze,
the living browns & greeneries
waving in the wind around me,
the real men & women
with whom I keep in touch,
our souls poking out

like bone
thru serious wounds,
the basic, familiar smell of life
raw or uncooked
breathed in thru nostrils
or exhaled thru tenderer membranes
— proof flowing back to me
that there's only one Dreamer:
the playful faddist & mystery lover
who sees me thru these boogies & tangos
whose steps & movements
seem to get made up
somehow as I go along

AUNT

She talks too loud, her face
a blur of wrinkles & sunshine
where her hard hair shivers
from laughter like a pine tree
stiff with oil & hotcombing

O & her anger realer than gasoline
slung into fire or lighted mohair
She's a clothes lover from way back
but her body's too big to be chic
or on cue so she wear what she want
People just gotta stand back &
take it like they do Easter Sunday when
the rainbow she travels is dry-cleaned

She laughs more than ever in spring
stomping the downtowns, Saturday past
work, looking into JC Penney's checking
out Sears & bragging about how when she

feel like it she gon lose weight &
give up smokin one of these sorry days

Her eyes are diamonds of pure dark space
& the air flying out of them as you look
close is only the essence of living
to tell, a full-length woman, an aunt
brown & red with stalking the years

POETRY

It is possible to rest here.
It is possible to arrive home
headed this way
thru the wind & rain of this night
alone
to a place where starlight
isnt the point.
It is true that we are orphans
under the skin
where fluids combine
& organisms function intelligently,
where vision or sound
in image or vibration
need only be true
to spark the way there.
There is here & always was.
You sniff & clear your throat
in this unintentional night
borrowed from eternity
or let yourself be saddened by nothing.
I sit in a white kitchen
next to the young walls,
yellow paper spread on yellow tablecloth,
& scratch helplessly,

wanting to take new leave
of the present
which was a gift,
longing to have known everything
& to have been everywhere
before the world dissolves
a tangle of journeys
& messages
unrecorded
undeciphered
wrinkled down into me.

BOOGIE WITH O.O. GABUGAH

O.O. Gabugah writes that he "was born in a taxicab right
smack on 125th and Lenox in Harlem on Lincoln's Birthday,
1945. Franklin Delano Watson was the name my poor brain-
washed parents gave me but I had that racist tag legally altered
once I got old enough to see what was going down. The O.O.,
by the way, stands for Our Own, i.e., we need to do *our own*
thing, can you dig it?"

In addition to being one of our strongest young Black
revolu tionary voices, Brother Gabugah is the author of half a
dozen volumes, all of which have appeared since last year.
Slaughter the Pig & Git Yo'self Some Chit'lins is the title of his
most popular work which is presently in its sixth big printing.
Other volumes include: *Niggers with Knives, Black on Back, Love
Is a White Man's Snot-Rag* and *Takin Names and Kickin Asses*.
His plays — *Transistor Willie & Latrine Lil* and *Go All the Way
Down & Come Up Shakin* (a revolutionary Black musical) —
received last month's Drama Authority Award.

The brother is presently the recipient of both a Federal Arts
Agency grant as well as a Vanderbilt Fellowship to conduct re-
search on Richard Wright. Currently vacationing in Aus-
tralia, he is preparing a collection of critical essays tentatively

titled *Woodpile Findings: Cultural Investigations into What's Goin On*.

His last critical work, *Nothin Niggers Do Will Ever Please Me*, is also a favorite.

"O.O. Gabugah draws strong folk poetry from the voice of a strident but vital revolutionary who attacks the Uncle Tom," states *The Nation* in its March 19, 1973, issue.

A militant advocate of the oral tradition, he chooses to dictate his poems through me rather than write them down himself.

— A.Y.

THE OLD O.O. BLUES

Like right now it's the summertime
    and I'm so all alone
I gots to blow some fonky rhyme
    on my mental saxophone

Brother Trane done did his thang
    and so have Wes Montgomery,
both heavyweights in the music rang,
    now I'mo play my summary

It's lotsa yall that thank yall white
    (ought I say European?)
who thank Mozart and Bach's all right,
    denyin your Black bein

Well, honkyphiles, yall's day done come,
    I mean we gon clean house
and rid the earth of Oreo scum
    that put down Fats for Faust

This here's one for-real revolution

where aint nobody playin
We intends to stop this cultural pollution
    Can yall git to what I'm sayin?

Sittin up there in your Dior gown
    and Pierre Cardin suit
downtown where all them devil clowns
    hang out and they aint poot!

We take the white man's bread and grants
    but do our own thang with it
while yall bees itchin to git in they pants
    and taint the true Black spirit

I'm blowin for Bird and Dinah and Billie,
    for Satch, Sam Cooke, and Otis,
for Clifford, Eric, and Trane outta Philly
    who split on moment's notice

Chump, you aint gon never change,
    your narrow ass is sankin
Like Watergate, your shit is strange
    You drownin while we thankin

My simple song might not have class
    but you cant listen with impunity
We out to smash your bourgeois ass
    and by *we* I mean The Community!

BLACK QUEEN FOR MORE THAN A DAY

I thirst for
    the Kool-Aid
   of your fabulous
fine fruit-flavored throat

Lick that ebony tongue
    out at me
    and let that licorice
    divine heavenly lickrish
      slide down my system

Chocolate mama, *mmm mmm*

Beauty is to boodie as
    class struggle is
      to ass struggle
    so let's git it on
for the night is long

When you place your hot dark arm
    cross my chest
    I'm like
some fierce tribal warrior
    ready to git
    down to natural bizness

With my head held high
    I walk through the sky
      with its cornrow of stars
    and you scroonched all
    up next to me
      sweet as you are

I'm the original poet
    (and I damn well know it)
      when you suckle me,
      you stallion you

Black woman
    my African Queen
      for more than a day
    kiss me with your
      Congo
        lips

WHAT YOU SEIZE IS WHAT YOU GIT

You must thank
  yo dookey don't stank
    while you be's gittin high
      up in the sky
of yo hand-
            ker-
              chief
                  head
        home, nigga,
  you sorryass muthafucka,
swillin slop at the white beast's
            trough
  (like black aint down enough),
    payin taxes insteada
      grindin axes,
slurpin up all that Boone's Farm
      Strawberry Hill
      (oughtta be called hell)
          wine,
  you wind-up, computerized
          Sambo

    You look like somethin
        outta Tarzan
  just cant wait to sniff Jane's titty,
        thinkin you pretty,
    but you aint nothin, nigga,
    you and yo old lady workin
      4 jobs 7 days a week
        & wont even speak
        up for yo rights
        day or night
    just so yo pickaninny chile
      can grow up and run the mile
      in the racist Olympics,
    oil for yall to slide for a ride
      on into the middle class

Well, all yall can kiss my revolutionary ass!

We tireda niggas buyin Cholly's wine and cars
  and neckties and bell-bottoms and yes books
  and bein bused to his plastic schools
  to learn how to be some white kinda fool

We talkin bout hackin the bleached-out devil
          to pieces
          & shippin Chunks-O-Hunky out to Venus
            for the interplanetary brothers
              up there to chaw on, muthas,
            you sassyass beautiful black muthas
              tryin to fare well on welfare

Quit playin with yo'self, nigga, & come!
  Come on back into the warm black fold
  that aint got nothin to do with gold

  Come on back where we at and *live*, i.e.,
    lib-er-rated, de-*live*-ered
          from tyranny!

  Come on back where we rezides
      greaze on some greens
      and check some sides —

      Shoot ol Pharoah
      (and we dont mean Brother Sanders)
    in the butt with yo poisoned Kikuyu arrow
  unless you tryna be the knee-grow Ann Landers . . .

      It still aint too late
      to keep the fate, Gate!

      Write on, Bruh,
    with yo funky baaaaaad-ass
        Afro-headed
        self!

                          Paris/Dar-es-Salaam, 1972

A POEM FOR PLAYERS

Yes, theyll let you play,
let you play third base or fender bass,
let you play Harrah's Club or Shea Stadium

Theyll let you play
in a play anyway: Shakespeare,
Ionesco, Bullins, Baraka, or Genet,
only dont get down *too* much
& dont go gettin too uppity

Theyll let you play,
oh yes, on the radio, stereo,
even on the video, Ojays,
O.J. Simpson, only please dont stray
too far from your ghetto rodeo

Theyll let you be Satchmo,
theyll let you be Diz,
theyll let you be Romeo,
    or star in *The Wiz*
but you gots to remember that
    that's all there is

Oh, you can be a lawyer or a medico,
a well-briefcased executive with Texaco;
you can even get yourself hired, man,
to go teach *Ulysses* in Dublin, Ireland

Theyll let you play
so long as you dont play around,
so long as you play it hot or cool,
so long as you dont play down the blues
theyll let you play in *Playboy*, *Playgirl*,
    or the *Amsterdam News*

Finally theyll let you play
politics if you dont get in the way
the way some of us did and had to be
iced by conspiracy, international mystery

Theyll let you play anybody but you,
that's pretty much what they will do

The Blues Don't Change
(1982)

HOW THE RAINBOW WORKS

for Jean Cook,
on learning of her mother's death

Mostly we occupy ocular zones, clinging
only to what we think we can see.
We can't see wind or waves of thought,
electrical fields or atoms dancing;
only what they do or make us believe.

Look on all of life as color —
vibratile movement, heart-centered,
from invisibility to the merely visible.
Never mind what happens when one of us dies.
Where are you before you even get born?
Where am I and all the unseeable souls
we love at this moment, or loathed
before birth? Where are we right now?

Everything that ever happened either
never did or always will with variations.
Let's put it another way: Nothing ever
happened that wasn't dreamed, that wasn't
sketched from the start with artful surprises.
Think of the dreamer as God, a painter,
a ham, to be sure, but a divine old master
whose medium is light and who sidesteps
tedium by leaving room both inside and outside
this picture for subjects and scenery to wing it.

Look on death as living color too: the dyeing
of fabric, submersion into a temporary sea,
a spectruming beyond the reach of sensual
range which, like time, is chained to change;
the strange notion that everything we've
ever done or been up until now is past
history, is gone away, is bleached, bereft,
perfect, leaving the scene clean to freshen
with pigment and space and leftover light.

MICHAEL AT SIXTEEN MONTHS

Ball	His whole world revolves around light dark
Bird	things sailing thru the air around chairs
Dog	the mystery of rising & falling & getting
Cheese	up again in the morning at night/scratching
Shoes	at windows to get out bananas oranges a
Cat	step/stepping down stepping up/keep the music
Juice	going/IV theme songs/walks on stories, dancing
Baby	on manhole covers, anything circular, objects
Daddy	that hang & flap in the breeze/the wind as
Mama	it foams into a room making the skin cool
Boat	puffing out curtains/baths/water/legs/kiss
Mama	Here we go into the rain turning sunlight
	Here we go down the slide into sandpiles
Mommy	Here we go clapping our hands as blocks fall
	Here we go running from Mama Mommy Mimi baby
No	crashing into Daddy dozing on the floor, a
	world is shooting out of rubber tree leaves
Nose	The window is a magic mirror/sad to see time
	flowing throwing itself thru flesh electric
Hot	that hard months ago was only a flash in
	a sea of possibility/the suffering afloat
Car	The meanness he will have to endure is only
	life ungathered in the eye of no world/is light
Book	pure & not so simple after all is living life
	alive alive O!

A SLEEPY DAY AT HALF MOON BAY

Like the shark who feels low but
frequent sound waves from afar
telling him it's dinnertime
somewhere under the sea,
I feel the pull of waves
splashing from my own center,
      softly, slowly —
lapping at my insides like a
long-forgotten dream that pops up
changed around years later,
more familiar & realer than noon

ARS POETICA

All that we did was human,
    stupid, easily forgiven,
Not quite right.
          Gary Snyder

Now that nothing has worked out
and the beautiful trees
are again in winter, feeding
on lean November light; the world,
like the cold, tentative yet tight
around his skin, his heart about
to pound right out of him,
he can linger on this corner again,
unnoticed, another dude in another street,
waiting for someone to keep an appointment
in the frozen belly of a large city,
no string quartets, no studio brass
bands to grace the meaningless background,
only the warmth of personal sun,

a blossoming peace stretching out.
In the soft folds of his brain —
she arrives as in a living photograph,
her everyday breath steaming the air,
warm under coat and sweater, simple
skirt, boots, the colored elastic of
her pants underneath snapped snugly
into place at the waist, at the thigh.

POEM WITH ORANGE

Finally you sit
at some table and put
your little life back
together again by
slicing a new orange

How closely the wet
glistening flesh of
this bright cut fruit
resembles all galaxies

How comfortably its
sweet pattern fits yours
as you watch each matching
diamond-juiced wedge
reaching, edging toward
essence, the center, home

FORT COLLINS, COLORADO

for Mary Crow

The present is a gift,
the past just a shift
in perspective balanced on thin air,
time sat out in a rocking chair

Neither of us knew those men
who made themselves at home here when
sky wasn't for sale and Denver
was a clean high clearing closeby, remember?

PEOPLE OF LETTERS

The mystery here in this paperweight world
is that anything of beauty gets written at all.
If poets are the unacknowledged legislators
of the world, then give me Benito Mussolini
who, tyrant though he was, made the trains run
on time, produced a bebop piano-playing son
and had no need of a penny-wise poet apologist.

Literary affairs may be likened to county fairs
or state fairs; theatrical events, the bigger
the badder, with carnival rides, bristling midways,
prize livestock, quilting bees, orchid displays,
pickled music, hot buttered corn and action booths
for streamered Chamber of Commerce concessions.
Unbusinesslike lovers of life had best just visit.

FOGGY MORNING

Disappearing around the comer
in his nylon red jacket with
the hood slipping from his hair
just brushed, my son trailing
gladness through clouds on the ground
waving to me that he can see the
yellow bus waiting for him up
ahead. Clutching his book, waving,
waving, with nothing but life.
I stand on the porch waving back,
a lump in my throat from moving
through the fog of my years that
sunshine is destined to dissolve.

NEW AUTUMN, NEW YORK

Late in the day when light is sandwiched
softly between slices of daytime and night,
I stroll around Gramercy Park, locked as usual
and all keyed up again for the real autumn.

To the falling of leaves in time-lapse slow
motion, I follow my feet, each crackling step
nudging me into a vaster present than this
friendly seasonal chill can circumscribe.

There is no end to the inward adventure of
journeying October to the edge of November.

A LITTLE POEM ABOUT JAZZ

for Miles Davis

Sometimes at the beginning of a movie
when they're flashing the title and heavy
credits over aerial shots of old New York —
skyscrapers that aren't really skyscrapers
because you'd have to be miles high to
see them that way on an everyday basis —
I think about *Green Dolphin Street* blown
over with wind and sound, and I picture
Elizabeth Goudge, whatever she looked like,
up on the stand with you, Trane and Cannonball,
a flower in her hair, a song in her throat.

THE ART OF BENNY CARTER

There are afternoons in jazz
when a leaf turns and falls
with so much barely noticed purity
that the not so secret meaning of
everything men and women have
tried to do beyond keeping afloat
becomes as clear as ocean air.

INTIMACY

Right up under our noses, roses
arrive at middleage, cancer blooms
and the sea is awash with answers.

Right here where light is brightest,
we sleep deepest; ignorant dreamers
with the appetites of napping apes.

Right this way to the mystery of life!
Follow your nose, follow the sun or
follow the dreaming sea, but follow!

CHEMISTRY

What connects me to this moon
is legendary, and what connects
the moon to me is as
momentary as the night is
long before it burns away like
that fire in the eyes of lovers
when, spent, they turn
from one another and fall against
the dark sides of their pillows
to let their blood color cool.

You too know well the nature of
our chemistry: 65% oxygen,
18% carbon, 10% hydrogen,
3% nitrogen, a touch of calcium,
phosphorous and other elements.
But largely (by 70%) we're water:
2 parts hydrogen to 1 part oxygen,
and mostly we're still all wet —

9 parts fear chained to 1 part joy.
Is this why we're given to drowning
ourselves in pools of tears,
long on sorrow and shallow on laughter;
drowning ourselves in sugar and salt
as it were, as we are, as the treasured
substance of a former fish's life
can never be technically measured?

This chemistry we swim and skim
is what connects all light with me
olympically, for real life
science will forever be proving
this radiant suspension to be love
in but one of its bubbling mutations.

BILLIE

Music: a pattern etched into time

I suck on my lemon, I squeeze my lime
into a bright but heady drink, soft
to the tongue, cold to touch, and wait

She who is singing enters my mouth,
a portion at a time: an arm, a leg,
a nipple, an eye, strands of hair—
There! Her song goes down and spins
around the way a toy pinwheel does, as
rosy blue blur, as rainbow, whirling
me through her throaty world and higher
Chug-a-lug enchantress, show me your
etchings. Warm me again now with
the red of your Cleopatric breath

IN MARIN AGAIN

for Arl

Again we drift back to these mountains, these
divine inclines our son could scale now.
Your loose blouse blows as you lean in worn jeans,
making it easy, a breeze to picture your breasts
underneath, your long legs: time's salty hello
still freely flowing after years of rainfall.
Smoothly we slip into this renewable night of
jagged crossings over dark peaks, fitful, fruitful.

Like mountains and rivers that go on and on,
love growing wild is wondrous, isn't it, with
its crazy horse catch-as-catch-can way of proving
that happiness, after all, is mostly remembered?

Love on the move encircles itself, boomerangs,
rounding out meaning the way water smooths stone.

MID-LIFE CRISIS: A CRITICAL REVIEW

Of course you will always want to be
in places where you are loved, even in
the middle of life, even in darkness,
that restless spot where childhood and
youth (so used to looking after you)
collapse, leaving you as vulnerable to
change as the song where you turn into
a one-eyed cat peeping in a seafood store.

What you really want, all you really need
is everything, absolutely everything and
to be by yourself until this storm blows over.

Yet left alone, you quickly become like a
fully grown zebra, snatched from its habitat
and shipwrecked in a zoo, straightjacketed
in your own skin whose shadows and bright stripes
tiger the burning noons and nights you stalk
like a self-jailed cellmate, solitary, confined;
you the turncoat, you the turnkey; eye to eye
with yourself at last, tooth to soothing tooth.

A SUNDAY SONNET FOR MY MOTHER'S MOTHER

for Mrs. Lillian Campbell

Consider her now, glowing, light-worn,
arthritic, crippled in a city backroom
far from the farm where she was born
when King Cotton was still in bloom.

She is as Southern as meat brown pecans,
or fried green tomato, or moon pies.

Gathering now for eight decades, aeons
of volunteered slavery soften her sighs.

Talk about somebody who's been there,
This grand lady has seen, remembers it all
and can tell you about anyone anywhere
in voices as musical as any bird's call.

Loving her, it hurts to hear her say,
"My grandchildren, they just threw me away."

FALLING ASLEEP IN A DARKENING ROOM

Blue, the most beautiful of afternoons
is to lie transfixed with pressure brought
to bear on your dozing zone, and then to
feel air being let out of the giant world,
a balloon big enough to live on but not live in
except perhaps to sleepers dreaming they're awake.

To lay you down to sleep with winter blowing
through rooms where you've been worrying too much,
run your engine's battery down to barely audible
palm-held miniature radio level . . . *Shhhhh* . . .

Now you can let laughter bubble out of silence
like kindergarten blobs of color flung against
emptiness, and let every unhurried passerby
become a painted shadow remembered in a slow dream
you always wanted to have, but haven't had yet,
not until now when, nodding, fading, you let go.

Everything you ever thought you were leaves you.
Alone, you wake up yesterday or maybe last week
or, fortunate, you fade back in, expanded again,
feeling virginal, refreshed — a new you not so blue.

W. H. AUDEN & MANTAN MORELAND

in memory of the Anglo-American poet & the
Afro-American comic actor (famed for his
role as Birmingham Brown, chauffeur
in those ancient Charlie Chan movies)
who died on the same day, September 28, 1973

Consider them both in paradise,
discussing one another —
the one a poet, the other an actor;
interchangeable performers
who finally slipped backstage
of a play whose cast favored lovers.

"You executed some brilliant lines,
Mr. Auden, & doubtless engaged our
innermost emotions & informed imagination,
for I pondered your *Age of Anxiety*
diligently over a juicy order of ribs."

"No shit!" groans Auden, mopping his brow.
"I checked out all your Charlie Chan
flicks & flipped when you turned up again
in *Watermelon Man* & that gas commercial
over TV. Like, where was you all that
time in between? I thought you'd done
died & gone back to England or somethin."

"Wystan, pray tell, why did you ever eliminate
that final line from 'September 1, 1939'? —
We must all love one another or die."

"That was easy. We gon die anyway no matter
how much we love, but the best thing I like
that you done was the way you buck them eyes
& make out like you runnin sked all the time.
Now, that's the bottom line of the black
experience where you be in charge of the scene.
For the same reason you probly stopped shufflin."

GOING BACK HOME

The burros are all heehawed out
The rum is gone and our friends with it
— 24 hours of pure loneliness
explained and joked and glanced away

The stars are out barking with the dogs
but flowers trees cornstalks and tomato
plants are fast asleep, chilled down in mist
We walk into town and argue and stare at
our cousins and nephews languishing in
produce stalls or under streetlamps in door-
ways and on the edges of taxi seats

Children play pinball and jockey machines,
their mothers and fathers clinking pesos
together late in the 20th Century mestizo night

We retreat to our lookout laid in the hills
with green invisibleness at this hour, down
our aspirin and vitamins B and C and walk
around the fireplace filled with wet wood,
newspaper and the dry hopes of the ages

With the aid of kerosene, soon there is
smoke rising up the chimney like light from
the village plaza below, reaching our window
with a choo-choo warmth as though there
were no such thing as Mexico or America,
only the lonely, naked spirits of people
shooting out of eyes and flesh, rambling
up these old mountains and back down again

WHAT IS THE BLUES?

Far away, I suppose you could say,
is where I'm always coming back from.
In any event it's where I want to be
— naked, undressable, inaccessible,
at the tip edge of the vanishing point.

Of course I keep thinking of throwing
in the towel but it isn't wet enough yet.
So, on a dare, I keep splashing around,
ducking down and coming up for air: my
tiny fair share of cool fulfillment.

And to vanish wouldn't be so bad.
Look at the visible, behold it slowly
and closely with unreddened eyes.
Without the stirrings of the heart
swimming in borrowed light, what could
we ever possibly lie down and see?

THE JAMES COTTON BAND AT KEYSTONE

And the blues, I tell you, they blew up
on target; blew the roof right off
& went whistling skyward, starward,
stilling every zooming one of us
mojo'd in the room that night, that
instant, that whenever-it-was. Torn
inside at first, we all got turned out,
twisting in a blooming space where
afternoon & evening fused like Adam
with Eve. The joyful urge to cry

mushroomed into a blinding cloudburst
of spirit wired for sound, then atomized
into one long, thunderous, cooling downpour.

What ceased to be was now & now & now.
Time somehow was what the blues froze
tight like an underground pipe before
busting it loose in glad explosions; a
blast that shattered us — ice, flow & all.
The drift of what we'd been began to
shift, dragging us neither upstream nor
down but lifting us, safe & high, above
the very storm that, only flashing moments
ago, we'd been huddling in for warmth.

Melted at last, liquefied, we became
losers to the blues & victors, both.
Now that he'd blown us away with his shout,
this reigning brownskinned wizard, wise
to the ways of alchemy, squeezed new life
back into us by breathing through cracks
in our broken hearts; coaxing & choking
while speaking in tongues that fork & bend
like the watery peripheries of time; a
crime no more punishable than what the
dreaming volcano does waking from what it was.

Believe me, the blues can be volatile too,
but the blues don't bruise; they only renew.

JUNGLE STRUT

in memory of Gene Ammons

Of all the nights, yours were greenest, Gene,
blue-breathing son of your boogie-bled dad
who, like you after him, left this dry world
a treasure tray of cocktails for the ear.

You loved making people high with your song
just as you must've loved soaring some yourself.
How high? Moon high, scaling neon heights like
an eagle humming along on silence and a bellyful.

Dumb hunters stalked you, staking you out shame-
lessly, especially when you were straddling air
pockets that, however turbulent, never blew away
your sound and rollicking command of flight.

The wine poured from your jug (when you weren't
locked up in one) was aging and tasty. Bottoms up!

MY SPANISH HEART

after Chick Corea

In audible dreams I'm forever going back
to Spain. Now, tell me what that's all about?
Perhaps in some past life or lives I lived
there and cared about the African presence
in Iberia or New Iberia, eh? Get serious!
It's probably because all my life I've been
an all-nite sucker for spicy rhythm ticking
and booming away like an afro-latinized gypsy
taxi meter waiting to be fed that long mileage.

Whatever the reason or rhyme, I can think of
no better fate than to end up masking my nights
m the gardens of Spain — and how Spanish is
Spain? — with a warm, bubbling, undreamed lady
whose dark-throated murmuring is song. Picture
it: Just a couple of music lovers, all but
wasting in moonlight, with poetry damp and cooling
right up under our noses, soft lips, a mustache
— Ay, the possibilities of Spanish, the loving
tongue! Listen . . . "Adiós, adiós, mi corazón."

LESTER LEAPS IN

Nobody but Lester let Lester leap
into a spotlight that got too hot
for him to handle, much less keep
under control like thirst in a drought.

He had his sensitive side, he had
his hat, that glamorous porkpie whose
sweatband soaked up all that bad
leftover energy.

How did he choose
those winning titles he'd lay on favorites
— Sweets Edison, Sir Charles, Lady Day?
Oooo and his sound! Once you savor its
flaming smooth aftertaste, what do you say?

Here lived a man so hard and softspoken
he had to be cool enough to hold his horn
at angles as sharp as he was heartbroken
in order to blow what it's like being born.

Al Young

THE BLUES DON'T CHANGE

> *"Now I'll tell you about the Blues.*
> *All Negroes like Blues. Why?*
> *Because they was born with the Blues.*
> *And now everybody have the Blues.*
> *Sometimes they don't know what it is.*
> Leadbelly

And I was born with you, wasn't I, Blues?
Wombed with you, wounded, reared and forwarded
from address to address, stamped, stomped
and returned to sender by nobody else but you,
Blue Rider, writing me off every chance you
got, you mean old grudgeful-hearted, table-
turning demon, you, you sexy soul-sucking gem.

Blue diamond in the rough, you *are* forever.
You can't be outfoxed don't care how they cut
and smuggle and shine you on, you're like a
shadow, too dumb and stubborn and necessary
to let them turn you into what you ain't
with color or theory or powder or paint.

That's how you can stay in style without sticking
and not getting stuck. You know how to sting
where I can't scratch, and you move from frying
pan to skillet the same way you move people
to go to wiggling their bodies, juggling their
limbs, loosening that goose, upping their voices,
opening their pores, rolling their hips and lips.

They can shake their boodies but they can't shake *you*.

By Heart
(1982–1985)

ALBA

Your insomniac sorrow settles
on the morning air like smoke
from stale cigarettes,
the pungent reminiscence of sadness
a questionable misadventure.
Night is nothing now except
the other side of what you thought
was real; a little bit like now.

You can sniff blues in the room,
floating out the opened summer
window, trailing what you thought
was you: the ancient dreamer
of a separate world, hard & solid
like some backstreet where spirit
never lurks or shows its face.
You're all but up & walking now;
still sniffing, nostrils flaring.

Outside sunlight's keeping the day
warm for you — a whole hour & a half
to go. Your alarm clock explodes.
You turn over, remembering how life
lived out an instant at a time is never
as sad as it seems in the dark.
In the subway gloom of sleeplessness
you race ahead of real time, real life &
what's left of yourself upon waking.

A POEM FOR OMAR KHAYYAM (1050?–1123? A.D.)

Humming like a hawk in motion,
high afternoon recedes,
flying back into the very hole of night
that was its birth canal.
O beautiful, dutiful womb
of arrivals and departures,
of light staying still
while our eyesight does the moving.
Day in, day out, this story
has its way of getting told.
In countless ways the days
spread their wings and fold.
I'm left out of the fold of time,
aching to release my useless
clutch and longing for the touch
that'll shatter the heart of matter.

Over the course of more midnights
and noons than I can hold in focus,
the terribly little I've learned is this;
that I, like the bird of time,
know almost next to nothing
except this living moment, feathered
with down, that sails up and away
with every palpitation of its breast.
The rest is pure deception in a sky
where Monday masqueraded as Friday
or Sunday passes itself off as Wednesday
at the tock of a clock. On moment's
notice the color of time's plumage
changes the way the beautiful changes
ring, seeming to chime wrong from right
but always mixing day with night.

The wing is on the bird, the bird is
on the wing. Neither makes sense
since never has there been anything

more airborne or flighty than this
eternal now I seem to keep calling
yesterday, tomorrow or intimate today.

REAL TIME

a birthday poem for Marj Pichon

When blue moons start to roll around
not once, not twice, but often
enough for old clichés to sound
profound, so wise they soften
the glare or brilliance of the sun
you thought you were at 20,
that's when you know the race is won.
You've reached the Beach of Plenty,
where insight looms and roams at large,
where your hardship sails in to dock;
you've conquered 40, Marj.
It's time to disconnect the clock
and simplify, and simply be
in love with life eternally.

SWEET SIXTEEN LINES

You bet it would've made a tender movie!
If only someone had been flighty enough
to capture the shape of what turned out to be
our last days alone, the end of a rough
journey that dulled every sense but touch.
Heroically juvenile, lighter than light,

we talked what we felt, but never thought much.
We were Romeo and Juliet night after night.
It was like we'd sailed from heaven in a jet,
copilots, cool but glorious, and landed
our sullen craft too artfully — poets yet;
runaways on life's slick runway of expanded
unconsciousness. Maybe. Who knows for sure?
But Ruby and the Romantics came out that year
with a sweet-nothing single: hot, airy and pure
enough to hold us aloft by heart and by ear.

A POEM FOR LENA HORNE

And when it came down to Negro nights,
those Colored Only slices in time,
you took the cake, Lena, & ran
& danced with it, O! You were so gorgeous
they didn't know what to do with you,
those not so gentle men at MGM & elsewhere.
Where else but in the USA's of the world
would it go on record that you & Ava
Gardner used to knock back a few
in the palmy hours, laughing over how
the studio would darken her up from head
to toe to lip-synch & mouth the sound
of your voice for *Showboat*. Hurray
for Hollywood! The jewel blue you will
never be seen, only heard in the role
of Miss Julie, the octoroon swooning
under the June-jazzed Dixiemental moon.

You can laugh about it now & soften the sting.
You can smile & even do a step or two & sing
& I suppose you haven't done bad, given
your class & origins & given the almighty odds

& the gods of showbiz heaven who own, control
& chart the color of beauty & its stars.
Tell me again about the time your numbers
banker daddy told Samuel Goldwyn he'd be happy
to pay for your maids & upkeep since
you didn't have sense enough to understand
the movies didn't have much use for people
of your hue. They stashed you in some doozies
too — *Panama Hattie, As Thousands Cheer,*
I Dood It, Swing Fever, Two Girls & a Sailor,
but the trick was to tailor you for the South.
How did they do it? Well, wasn't much to it.
They'd log you in, then chop you out (like
lumber) for the slumbering southern houses.

I knew your son Ted, a fledgling writer, dead
to you these many years. You outlived him,
your husband and your dad who all moved out
in the very same year. I can almost hear —
sometimes when you sing — the strong & lasting
side of you that once told Billie Holiday
she had to learn to be tough, that these hucksters
didn't mean no man no good, let alone womanhood.

You're still lovely, Lena. Moms Mabley was wrong.
The rubberbands she said were holding your face up
are never going to snap. You are the song.

WHY A HUSH SHOULD NOT BE RUSHED

In the push of time, it's all too easy
to overlook the ineffable,
the intoxicating quality of everything
that is; the way old patterns of seeing
blind us to what is framed right
before our bleary eyes. Heartbeat
by heartbeat, universes are blooming
and decaying with the tide
of every breath that takes our death away.
The world of look is finally a mirror
we breathe upon in our own sweet time.

HOW STARS START

I don't ask to be forgiven
nor do I wish to be given up,
not entirely, not yet, not while
pain is shooting clean through
the only world I know: this one.
This is no Mal Waldron song or
Marlene Dietrich epic in black
& white where to scrawl against
the paradigms of time is to mean
something benign, like dismissing
present actions or behavior because
I know & understand deep down
inside & beyond that life itself
is acting all of this out; this
kamikaze drama, cosmic if you
will, but certainly comic, in a style
so common as to invite confusion.

Who am I now? What have I become?
Where do we draw the line between being
who I am and what I ought to be?
Need is a needle, nosing its sticky load
into my grief, spilling into veins
that can't be sewn, transforming their dark
cells into lighted semblances of relief.
The stomach is involved; flesh itself;
memories of an island doom that leaves
no room for sense or sensitive
assessments of truth about myself.
Which is the me that never changes?

All roads lead back to starts, to where
I started out, to stars: the fiery
beginnings of our ends & means; our
meanness & our meanings. There never
was a night begun in darkness,
nor a single day begun in light.

SAUDADES: THE PORTUGUESE BLUES

Perched at the railing of a Portuguese
freighter, frightened inside, wavelengths
from home and known to no one here
except the not so secret police,
I'm struck by how that brownskinned girl
in a moon-knit dress and Sunday pumps
beams from the pier below. Already I know
next to nothing about her, and soon
I'll know even less. But nothing
could've possibly prepared me for her
long-distance smile that gently bridges
the mileage anywhere. How can I not be
gladdened by sharing the way she shines

in the late Lisbon night; a quivering
blue glow seeping into the deep
and rolling sea? Just see how she sways
and waves at the sight of her father
the seaman, the ship's wireless operator
positioned just now at my left, right
beside me. He's back in contact
with his proudest connection: this
motherless angel he's been bragging about
like a daddy all the way over from steamy
Brooklyn to the shores of the Azores, and
on to the mainland and islands of me.

Shaken to discover myself so removed
from all the family I've ever known,
I couldn't be happier than I am now,
watching him hurry down the gangplank home.
They charge into each other's arms and then,
peering up, squinting, shading his eyes,
he signals me his last farewell. Ah, well,
this is where I become a stranger again;
an unraveled, woolly-minded, off-season
traveler all decked out with no place else
to go and no one to answer at these ports
of call. Soon we'll be free to be memories
of each other. But for one skylit minute —
radiant and radio clear — another part
of my head snaps on; it begins to crackle
with a pop song from long ago about kisses
and fundamental things. And time and I
go drifting by; we flow with the last
of the cool, salty light out across
the dark dock water that cradles this
crusty old boat. In fact, as I shoulder
my pack of belongings, a longing
overcomes me and for chorus after chorus
I can still feel that flow; feel it
pulling us apart; feel it nudging
the swollen summer toward fall. Sighing,

descending now; I can even feel how time
will feel as it lightens my momentary
burden of being all too young, all too
wise, and far too deliriously alone.

HOUSTON IN OCTOBER

Or is really October in Houston?
There's no telling anymore; nor
does it matter that the moon,
two-thirds on the wane, yet perfectly
sane, belongs in a Texas song tonight.

I love the way she's still the moving
moon; love the slow, glowing quickness
of her golden disappearing act.
The mood she sets in this drenching
orchid heat is sisterly & southern.

Locusts bunched in trees & Spanish moss
broadcast their mating calls of longing
on electromagnetic cycles so powerful
they short-circuit the tropical meaning
of this steaming night & even subdue
the city's oil-rich evening aurora.

But there's no getting around it —
the whirring of cicadas in this deep-sea
Houston heat assails, propels &
sends me sailing toward cooling memories
of a lazy, fanning kind; memories
of a helicopter, yes, buzzing belly up,
suspended by a ladder to the moon.
It is the power of this whir that stirs
the stubborn air with whistling karate-chop

precision, that magnetizes all sounded
light within earshot of its ups & downs.

Yes, it's this sweaty, moon-fed chirping
that draws the drowsiness from October
over & over & over again until I slip
deep enough into sleep to see my day
for what it's been; to soak all over
again. I dream in green & silver.
Drained like the cicada & glad as any
spent songster who knows how to take
a fall, I cool my heels and let go.

A SINGULAR YEN

The craving for infinity
may begin at any time.
It struck me first in Berkeley
in a dark, troubled time
I confused it with affinity.
The second time it overcame
me was in Houston, Texas
in another stormy tryst,
only this time clouds
parted long enough for me
to see with painful lucidity
what it was I had to do
& where I had to go
to satisfy this singular yen.

After all these years
of toying with realness,
of playing with the ace,
my truth of it has hit home,
arriving like light on time.

I swallow & stumble
into the awesome center
of this sun wave unafraid,
looking to get straight once
& for all, knowing I must
go with the infinite altogether,
against every shimmering odd.

SENTIENCE

As for the hawk, what grander bird
can you cite with more authority than
this beak-eager flyer of life delivered
like a package that is itself the gift
wrapped deep within. Hawks talk, yes,
& so do doves, but the dove is slick.
Doves, you see, having weathered all
kinds of nights that've enjoyed themselves,
aren't interested in talk in the least;
dreaming's their thing. They don't even sing.
They lie or fly or flit around or fling
their wings in the direction of the moon
that gives them their open-aired color.

A BRAND NEW MORNING LOVE SONG

Maybe I shouldn't but I must tell you
about a very old love blowing back
into my life for what feels like forever
at last. She looks however I wish
her to look, yet always it's the eyes,

those violet, violet eyes of hers
so electrically intense at times they glow
& even buzz in the dark with deep feeling
like the magic of those oldtime gypsies
putting across their passionate flamenco
numbers vibrant with catchy cries & steps.
And everytime I slip she catches me
not so much in her crazy arms as
in the fragrant center of her being
whose strength & breadth surpasses
any earthly fire fighter's rescue net.
I leap without a thought of where I'll land
into watery, smoke-filled air without alarm
& know she'll be there waiting everytime.
Her whisper is enough to dowse the flames.
And everytime I slip up she corrects
my errors eagerly like a wise & caring sister.
She whispers in my ear secrets I can barely
make out until in the thick of some crisis
a light clicks on. You see, the price is
always right, for her advice is free & freeing.
She'll meet me more than halfway anyplace
I choose & all it costs is touch. Is this
too much to ask of any lover, especially
one who powers my every waking hour with songs
only I can hear even in that wildest of wildernesses:
the snarled & brambly jungle of my jumping heart?
There is no night or day when she's around;
only the quivering, quintessential nowness
of her realness; the feathery touch of her lips
against my heated forehead is enough
to make my sleepy eyes fly wide open
& fill me with the urge to sing of her alone.

SELECTRIC II

The impeccable is possible
& more than peckable on this
handsome instrument unveiled
to fashion sound & sense
out of silence from the inside
of nowhere way down here
in the sunny Southland where
it's been raining four straight
days. I love the way the words
correct themselves, the way
my laughing cables compose themselves
as we go zipping along.

O don't tell me modernity
isn't without its maternal
aspects: Clean & shapely
specks of night-black ink,
as plastic as time or space,
splatter in lines across the page
at the tap of a finger, making
music that way; ready to be
restored to emptiness
the very minute meaning rambles
or goes wrong or slyly awry.

This baby is its own mother.
See how gracefully she picks
herself up, sets herself down
& starts all over again like
colorly clay in a rainstorm.

The only face she can't erase is space.
Here's to her motionless carriage;
the electrifying hum of her voice.
I'm right at home in my element now.

JANUARY

The VW needs serious transmission work,
the Datsun blows a radiator hose,
Blue Cross wants $425 right away,
the last checks of December come back
bouncing off the wall at $8.50 a crack,
the turntable quits spinning,
mildew overtakes the bathroom walls,
there's $50 worth of developed pictures
at Fotomat you can't afford to pick up,
the old typewriter's gonna cost $30
to fix up so you can rent it out.
You bite into an apple & hurt your molar
on the stem the same molar with root canal
work done last January & it's time
to go in for a checkup. They're gonna kick
you outta the screenwriters guild if
you don't pay up the 2 years' back dues.
The City of Los Angeles owes all
the money you spent in travel costs
to do a gig way back in November,
the radio you bought your son for graduation
fell apart & it's cheaper to buy a new one
than have his fixed, the Xmas briefcase
your wife gave you its handle's slipped off
already, prospects keep growing colder
as the water you're in grows hotter.
You know it's January when you have to stop
& pay close attention to what you're doing
wrong that seemed O so right last July.

AMERICAN TIME

You know you've come back home again
when they start snatching plates
right out from under you in restaurants
before you get to savor all your food;
there is no time, there just isn't time.
The country of mad hatters, this is
that; the Wonderland it took a mathematician
with a penchant for myths and nymphets to imagine
the way it truly is: Hello/Goodbye/Drop me
a line/Let's grab a bite/Give us a ring/
Damage estimated at six million dollars/
Instant replay/Times Square squared/Everything
you ever wanted in a beer and less/rushes
and rushes and rushes of early returns —
there is no time, there just isn't time.

You know you've come back home again
when you turn up at the office on Sunday
morning to find the trees that stood
in front of the building only yesterday
have been dug up and hauled away so clean
you think you've lost your mind. But what
about the stores shut down since you've been
gone and the buildings leveled and the whole
blocks excavated to leave you standing
frozen in your tracks trying to remember
in January what had been there in December?
And the neighbors who casually say, "Oh, hey,
the moving van'll be here Saturday, we forgot
to tell you we're pulling up stakes for Oregon."
Computerized dating, Disneyland waiting,
queues and cues and oolyacoos of twisty bebop
drop you constantly into to-be-continued
new waves of slaving variations on a theme.

THE OCTOBER VARIATIONS

1

October slows thru me
like a warm old song,
cooling the passageways
of my light-thirsty cells.
It all stands out in living
blue like a vein of sky
bursting with anticipation
of the hit of joy it is
about to receive in this month
of cool Sundays & Saturdays
& freewheeling Fridays.

2

Love, I know you now,
know you best of all
in October when we meet
openly under the green turning
blue of blonde on blonde leaves,
or in the blazing red & brown
of close-by fields, tumbling
always somehow among the pumpkins.

3

You put on any mask you want
but I'd know you anywhere.
Sometimes you come to me
disguised as May or September
but I'm too young to be fooled
by such old folks' pranks.
All I do is look into the cold
mirror of your morning eyes
where the whole day waltzes
& naps in vivacious detail

as crisp & clear as a shiny new
shoot of shadow leafing it
thru the garden of all my cares.
There's something gorgeous
about the seed I plant in you,
October, or is it all & only you
flashing in the light of your own
beauty, so clear, so sharply in focus
you could easily break into flame
from heat at the heart of you.
I can vouch for spontaneity, but
the combustion's all yours-in-bloom.

4

In the Seattle of loneliness
October is a dream, but Houston
can take that dream & walk & bike
around inside it the way Ann Arbor
used to do on football Saturdays
beyond the stadium. In Italy
I can easily picture you again —
October of narrow streets, slyly reaching
over beaches to steal little feels
of the runaway sea. Green October,
marbled October of the mountains
sloping down across unfarmed fields
drowsy with the wine light of Tuscany.
You're like an orange & bubbling aria
spreading your sound across the air
until every ear by turns turns autumnal.

5

Flat-nosed October,
October of the sleek cheekbones
pulled up high like Asia
in the Navajo universe;
a blood-reddening season

with frost-like salt rubbed
into your wounds; the reason
for eyes that sulk & charm
like big clipped moons of chance.
October game, October flame unblanketed
— the very press of your broad
belly & winter-ready breasts
against my summer weariness
is enough to shoulder all the joy
of your black hair spread out &
starry in this cold smile of a night.

6

Bag ladies in other New Yorks
know October from scratch.
They know the bloated foot
of you & that nasty taste;
know you as flukes & catches.
To get out of you all they can,
these women often think of ways
to coax you up to make-believe
rooms they own inside themselves;
rooms where they can nurse
you back to August health &
pat the scary pinkness from your face
until you look June-like again.
To them October means November is
about, biding its subway time,
harboring mean, slashing December.
So why not make peace with sober
October? Why not kidnap it
clean like a hungry dreamkeeper?

7

People look at each other differently
in October than they do, say, in May.
Between men & women there's a sad laughiness

in the early morning workaday workaday world
& among women a playful, furry caring.
But for men unto themselves in October
there's that little boy rejoicing;
there's a quality of innocence, the quality
of merciful lifetimes spent spinning
worlds that were never June, never
January, never December, but always October,
holy October of the gods drunk on light
& the wine of winter coming. So sleep late
Saturdays & don't go looking a rascal
in the eye; you just might catch his disease
or her perversion or, staring October
in the eye, you might get sucked
into the leaf-burning sweetness of eternity.

TOTAL INCANDESCENCE

for Ann Hinkel

I owe you this picture:
In some soon-to-be room,
maybe the very one you
find yourself in now,
your mouth will fall open
& out of it will pour
springtimes of silence.

I'm thinking about light whirling
around & around you & from
within & away from you, jamming
the spatial veinworks of all
your special, spacious being;
light moving up your spine
at 186,000 miles a second

& straight out the top & bottom
& back & front of you, radiating
forever like that, washing clean
& clearing the way for what
you're going to learn again &
again in this soon-to-be room
which is, in fact, already
twinkling in your blood.

AVAILABLE LIGHT

for Ann again

At Ann's place, even before you arrive
everything's OK, everything's peaceful.
The apartment air is impregnated with peace
particles. Picture her smiling as she looks
into the mirror to your soul: the eyes,
beam to beam, as she explains why thoughts
are things and how they work. Or picture
her giddiness when she walks into the living
room, carrying a tray of tea and cookies,
saying, "This is called yerba mate; it's pretty
good." Then, lighting candles and putting on
Paul Horn's solo flute musings, she laughs.
Inside the Pyramid is where our meditation
begins this time around. Later she laughs again
and explains why she's limping, says,
"I took a fall, a double somersault night
before last on my way up to Glenn's house.
You know that wobbly wood railing that leads
up to his front door — well, I slipped
on the steps and — whew! — Glenn told me
I missed my calling, said I shoulda been
an acrobat!" So she's hobbling tonight.

Last month it was her knee that got knocked
out of joint. This is the woman who teaches
the Star Exercise and other yogic stances;
who's teaching us about the limitless powers
of mind and soul and who we really are
deep within this pyramid of body, mind and soul.
She leans back in her chair, pats her short
coiffed hair and listens to everything
each of us says, even when we all talk at once.
Often she feels our thoughts as they circle
the steam-heated room, before they pass
through the prisms of her lighted windows
to whirl around the world and hover there
either as sunshine or as clouds in the endless
sky. O the roof of true, infinite love
is so vast it can only be housing eternity!

Once we walked from her place on Powell Street
to a Taoist vegetarian restaurant in Chinatown.
I held Ann's hand as we managed a worldly hill.
She huffed, puffing great frosty rings
of breath in the chilled San Francisco twilight,
but all the way her fingers pulsed with warmth.
For the very first time it occurred to me
how this beautiful woman was approaching
her 75th year on earth with humor and with wit
and knowledge; still years younger than us.
"I sometimes enjoy a good hamburger," she said
when I asked if she were strictly vegetarian.
And the light, it pours from her heart of hearts
and spills upon children like us who keep seeking
her out. It's the same light that plays
around her peaceful visage when she speaks
or sighs or sits to breathe in silence, or breathe
the glowing sound of warm bamboo in easy repose.
She's the very mother we've all always wanted.

AFTER VISITING ARL AT THE HOSPITAL

Poetry
like a bent ray
of light
returns
to these crumbling
portals to find
me still at home
if not at ease
& the message
she brings is joyous to receive

Keep moving, she says
Don't ever give
up your search
for the true home
we're heir to;
palatial omnipresence
that begins & ends
everywhere or no place
according to how
you choose to live or see it

The flower in this
vase before me now
not only smiles
but winks,
leaking out
the same message
except in flower
language message is
sentiment; warm
& sometimes all wet
like a puppy

The very sky laughs
at me, saying, See
you go around

& around feeling
sorry for yourself
when all the while
you're being whisked
thru space & up
above appearances
to learn all over
again that you're nothing
if not spirit
dreaming its otherness
dreaming bent rays
of light returning
like poetry

LIGHTNING, DIVINE LIGHTNING

And what do you say
when the drift of summer
explodes & keeps exploding
in thunderstorms of August rain?
Is it proper to ignore what is
obvious: the lightning voice
of a divine sky mother
who speaks to you repeatedly,
heatedly in ways you've never
been spoken to before; in flashes
of silence ionized to an ash
before your very ear & eye?

When you are a frozen piece
of that divinity who follows you
from California to Italy,
from land to land & sky to sky
leading you across oceans
back to the desert of your dreaming:

Tucson, Arizona, do you write that
off serenely in the sands & mists
of time? Or do you recognize
this sky of skies as the very you
connecting yourself all over again
to rain, to the inner meaning
of thunderous downpours & giant nights?

Writing in the sky is as much
yours as the reader is you. The touch
of this electric blue deity's beauty
is a zigzag reminder of wholeness.

MOVING, MERGING, FADING, STANDING STILL

in memory of my mother,
Mary Campbell Simmons
(1922–1982)

There's no way you can know how it begins,
this dialogue, this conversational
bridge between sons & mothers, mother & son.

It must be quiet where you're sitting now,
or walking beside some stream the picture
of nothing we've got around here, not quite,
& yet it's hard to think of you adrift in space
without a background, some façades to highlight
the necklace of your smile, the soft turn
of your other cheek or eye or both; the sun-
light of your inner self waylaid & pinned
down at last in a timeless, spaceless place
where it must be as easy to transmit pictures
as it is here to run one's mouth like they do
Downsouth. Tell me what after-world you're in,

you who longed to move among the sumptuous
& pass your nights above all cities' lights.

Tell me in that low and changeable country voice
what restful field you're sunning in now,
the ground beneath you as green as a grin
of somebody who doesn't know what they're doing
but that's OK because they love it, they love it.

No more changing of hospital linens, no more
gardening from dawn to night, no more trying
to figure out what made your kids so sad,
no more Stompin' at the Savoy of your racing heart
on fire with queenly possibilities; no more shoes
& no more blues & no more going to market with just
a basketful of nerves & gathering smarts.

Sometimes I see you as you were when I was three,
plucking still-sweet chewing gum from your mouth
& offering it to Frank or Billy or me,
always on the move & moving on. I'm listening
to Pachuta, Laurel, Ocean Springs, Chicago,
Detroit, Milan, L.A., Hot Springs & New York;
listening to the way the cities & the towns keep
running away from one another, moving, merging,
fading, standing still like your breath must have
done that morning in the hospital once we'd talked
& I'd said something about telephoning all the kids,
& you said, "Don't waste your time, call God.
Call God if you just got to go callin', call God!"

Clean, whistling thru my mediations, comes
the sound of you telling me that & more;
the look in your eye I'd seen in laetrile Tijuana
by the sea, a look that had already glimpsed
a place far away, a place I thought about down
in Australia at the gateway to my forties,
never in my dreaming wildness knowing
you weren't about to get past 60 years.

There's no way you can know how it begins,
this monologue that wants to take off on life
& so-called death. You're calling me & I'm
about to answer in a language, on a frequency
beyond the range of cancer & its cures. My voice
breaks down the skies of silence to your star.

IMPROVISATION

There's something or maybe even
nothing about an old session
existing in snarls of tape alone
that sets the ears on fire & the heart
fluttering tall & alluvial, loosening
that barely grounded undertow of quick
sand: Man: the measure of all fullness.
Think of God, think slowly of God
holding all of Creation in the most durable
yet delicate of suspensions, letting go
with constellations of bliss, hard-packed
smatterings of the marvelous it might take
aeons to understand or unravel, much less
experience, & to think that in each moment
we're experiencing the whole of eternity
piecemeal, as though you were to scoop
a handful of water from the ocean.
There in your imperfect vessel of a hand,
slipping thru your fingers, is the ocean
in miniature; a drop in the bucket of love.

INVITATION

in memory of Papa Jo Jones
& Philly Joe Jones

There'll be all the requisites
& O how exquisite
the presence of night blooming
jazzmen & women, flowering
in aurora borealis like all the rounded
midnights & Moscow nights & New Delhi
dawns you ever wanted to drop in on
or sit in with or pencil
into your calendar of unscheduled delights.

There'll be love in all its liquid
power, rhythmic & brassy; mellifluous
forms, flashing flesh & the slippery
glittering skin of your teeth;
enchantment, male & female;
the orchid chords of hothouse scat
as pop song, as darkness sweetened
with light; the ascension of steps
that lead to some sumptuous Park
Avenue apartment where a bemoanable lady
lives, sophisticated to a fault, in need
of this bittersweet cultural chocolate,
this quiescent sensation of an invitation.

It'll be big, this gig called life;
the biggest. Johann Sebastian Bach
knew what it was like to bop
through a shower late in the afternoon,
then hang out in your hotel/motel/do-tell
room, wondering what time it really is
back in Iowa City or New Orleans or
the New York of all New Yorks or Rome,
the home you just left the way
autumn leaves — suddenly. Or now it's Paris

where it's going to be wine & cold sandwiches
while you're longing to dine on collard greens
& blackeyed peas with ribs & sauce
hot enough to burn away the sauerkraut &
pig's knuckle of international loneliness.

You'll make your calls & sail off
into an aria or a deep tocatta; in short
you'll honor the invitation your heart
has cabled you direct from the ace,
fulfilling all those requisite licks
so exquisite to the crowd whose deafening roar
will silence all the circus lines
the blue-hearted you never got to deliver.

It'll be the liver of life within who'll know
how *répondez s'il vous plaît* should play.
Just plan to sit & make yourself at home.

JAZZ AS WAS

Sometimes it's the flagrant accentuation
of bebop & late afternoon loneliness
that devastates; those early night
hours just don't get it, so everything
that happens long past midnight grows
misty with whiskey & other forms
of practiced behavior. The drummer's
got some new white girl on hold who adores him.
The piano player's totally clean but
won't comb her hair; she's hip to the bone.
The bassist is a communist the way
he scribbles off accompaniment like a giant
bear waltzing africally thru bureaucratic
steps. Hey, it's America heard in rhythm

& enormous harmonies the color of October;
swollen & falling, full of seedy surprises
that make your hoary heart speed up
& do double time between the born-again beats.

BY HEART

The leaves on the trees,
the smell of the ocean,
the feel of the earth —
we sit embalmed in lonely clubs
at night, remembering this,
feeling sorry for ourselves
when all the time God is
whispering and zinging
along the telephone wires
of our secret hearts,
telling us, "I love you,"
showing us how. And yet
we shut that soft voice out
like the wind in a leaky cabin.
We know all this by heart
but we forget until the singer
makes the insides of us tremble
like the leaves on the trees,
then suddenly we smell the ocean
and feel the earth whirling
around and around the worlds
of lazy space between our thoughts.

PROCESS

From looking at things Navajo
& Native American, I am learning
to re-picture all that lies around
& within me as process; as step
by step I come to understand
where we go wrong when we cling
to the notion of there being
such things as fixed objects that
exist outside of ourselves in some
external world of which we are only
momentarily a part because of our
ability to perceive, that's all.

No, perception itself is process.
The thing perceived & the perceiver
are one; everything is in flux,
subatomic particles are dancing
by the trillions on the stump of your
big toe; subtle radiation bombards us
everytime we remember that universes
reside within a glistening slice of
seeded red-green-neutral-almost-white
watermelon cut from its vine & harvested
from a specific patch of earth where
the sun shines down & cool nights come.

And where do we come from? Clearly
there's something exciting & mysterious
going on here; something or, rather,
some process of enchantment so vast
& giddying that we're moved to turn
our backs on it & go to movies instead.
One glance at the sea is more than we
can handle. Snap a picture & let's go!

WHATEVER BECOMES OF THE LIVING?

for Kenneth Rexroth,
in memoriam

By the sea it was, the Pacific,
your eyes glazed with dream
& the sonorous Indiana of your voice —
part ponderous, part invention — you
blinked & looked hard at me
the first & second times we met
at Asilomar then at Santa Cruz,
each setting the perfect location
for a moving star like you, like
the Santa Barbara that saw you slip
away into the blue of another home.

What happens? Whatever becomes
of the living? Your voice still graces
unaccountable passages of my rites
en route to poethood. I have as much
right to look on you as teacher
as anyone raising themselves
in the razor winds of my catch-all,
stormy era. But there is no sound
sharp enough to cut through the water
& the thunder of you flashing
in your own shrewd role as soul publicist,
as worldly Hoosier booster of the spirit-feel.

MORE CLUES TO THE BLUES

Sometimes it's the way the blues hits you
that matters, that shatters you safely
like soft rock hurled against auto window glass.
Nothing really flies & nothing ever dies
except the engine of enjoyment as it skips
& turns over at the wrong speed, in the wrong
gear, just enough to set your fabulous teeth
on edge like an invisible vibration you can't spell.
That's when the blues can get in the way, can
waylay the very course of your soul & divert
its streams of quiet screams inward to a place
where energy & emotion are equally picturable.

It can hit you down by the docks in Singapore,
or at a desolate crossroads in wintry Mississippi,
or on Cottage Grove in a Chicago that never goes
away, or in the depths of New Delhi, or just outside
Grants Pass, Oregon, where the sheriff sits
at the counter, sunglassed, checking out the strange
new nigger in town, you, with guns on his hips
& a snarl on his lips, or in the suburbs of Paris
after some Marxist marksman of a Frenchman brags
to you of La France et la liberté & then kicks
or curses a Moroccan the way a Dutchman might
a Surinamese, or an Aussie, an aboriginal Arunta.
The blues is encroachment; a mental state of being
the very people upon whom roaches rush in to feed.

YOUR BASIC BLACK POET

He mounts the stand &
people turn colors

Where in the world
could he be coming from?

What can he tell us new
about the racial situation?

Why are there oceans in
his poems, sunshine, glacial
journeys toward reunion?

What's the matter with
his diction man he
sho dont sound that black?

Now if he was from Johannesburg,
better yet from Mozambique
or even from St. Martin's
it would be easier to relate
all them drumbeats & bananas
in his blood with the sun
pounding down & around,
that Afric look a sound.

Anyway if he was for real
he'd be off chasing flies
way out in left field or
recovering a broken jaw
from a bigtime heavyweight bout,
off into Ghanaian ghettoes,
revolution rapped in a gown.

Any way you look at it
the dude is irrelevant,
& dangerous to the community.

THE ONLY RACE THERE IS

I can't keep up with your love anymore,
coming as it does at me in storms
& playful, sunny cascades; the thrill
of being in your world undermines
every effort I make to keep pace.
Turning it all over in my heart,
sometimes I feel I'm getting started
again, coming back, regaining. But
O the endlessness of your surprises,
sprung below me in zero cities where
I thought I'd die when breath
froze in my lungs, & in ridiculous
washes of rain like in watercolored
Seattle where I settled for big
moments in space, & in the desert,
the Arizona desert of lightning storms,
high kitchen heat & crystalline silence —
you, you, you, you, nobody but you
wrap your pliant night & daytime arms
around me until I'm smothered again
in the forest of your green, high touch.
The mountain of you, the oceanic
depths; the cutting, starlit pointillism
connecting all the dots from pinpointed
initial space to vast refrigerated milkiness
of your ways. The days grow lighter
& lighter & longer & longer when I'm walking
or thinking of you, love; you who will
always lay down more than I could ever
pick up; in vast, ringing, invisible stretches
& hunches that parachute me back into myself
in silvery circles of giddiness, laughing
while I slowly learn to let go & let you
uphold this, your world. I give it all back,
by the way. Who wants to run with the runner?

After all it's your race, your unbroken record.
All I want to do is hang around the stands,
lit up, like a slow, whirling fan all aglow.

THE PHYSICS OF LONELINESS

Translate this into higher math
if you can: One window away
from here the sun is glinting
off the pane like a visual echo
of eternity & the only way
to grasp it completely is with eyes
shut tight like a darkened door.

There's no other recourse, absolutely
no harking back to a simpler picture;
only this concentration of straight,
unfiltered, unadulterated light
let loose against this blast
of gleaming glass — clearly far too
much for any after-work weekday mind
to clutch for long; not on an empty
stomach, not when coming home
to an empty apartment has driven you
slowly to the brink of lightlessness.

A bulb snaps off in your solar plexus
& suddenly you want to be that beam
of blinding, circular energy illumining
the symmetry & variety of appearances.

HOBOKEN BROKEN DOWN:
A HASTY RECOLLECTION

It was Hackensack, no, Hoboken, the town
I spent creaky subway rides from the lowest
Manhattan to get to, and why was that?
Hey, it wasn't Frank Sinatra pulling me there!
It wasn't the jukebox Mafia or the sailors
just in from Italy either, nor was it
Paul Goodman who was spending the summer
of 1963 there where the young would visit.
I think, looking ahead, it might've been
the pressure was off & there was no way back
to myself except to take off & leave the Earth
by burrowing deep into the salty rushes
of green & warmth & stubble & broken Italian
glass & Puerto Rican chickens — cold so far
away from San Juan roots — & O the juicy
dribble of those late night roasted snacks;
better than *shaishu bau* (cheap pork buns)
at the dumbwaitered Ho-Ho Dinette on Mott Street,
the Chinese White Tower of its day.
Were we crazy, were we nuts? You bet we were.
You can't tell anything actual about the past
without making it up, really, even though
you got names & dates & places to go by.
We're forever setting out to map & trap
the now of our no-whereness & settling for the gone.
Long ago in a summer of beer & discovery,
I treasured the lushness of just being able
to sneer back at Manhattan from Jersey.

A POEM FOR WILLARD MOTLEY

Sometimes at the mouth of this river,
from the far right side of my brain,
I fish all night
in Mexican remembrance
of you, Willard Motley; your elegant
hoodlums, your cinematic wops
trapped by themselves between mid-
night and dawn inside air bubbles
no fish could ever fill
with sly, spicy cartoon talk.
I don't suppose you had to be
womanless or manless to cast
such virulent lines into the mouths
of your violent, somnolent characters
but I'd be willing to bet
a Kentucky Derby to a Frank Yerby
that fearlessness helped.

Your forget-me-not bohemian ways
live on in the slow memory
of someone who only heard
about your private, festive outbursts
in a sea-surrounded salt & tequila land
the abrupt & unnameable color
of the fathomless dreams of our race.
And so sometimes at the muddy banks
of these waters I stand & unreel
my own knotted lines; a knucklehead
shadowed in silver light & weary
as Bogart of knocking at doors.

Again & again I picture John Derek,
the way he was: your firstborn
prettyboy screen-heroic victim
whose latest wife Bo played Jane
to a Tarzan I couldn't even stick
around the theater long enough to see.

My eyes were too lidded with sad, rusting
ironies to stay open in the heavy-colored
dark. Somehow I couldn't stop
thinking about Fred Astaire,
that agile, singing step-dancer
the whole world loved up there.
After all the riches Negroes paved
his way with, how could he go &
marry that frisky young jockey
of a wife who openly championed the KKK?

It's a very old story, you know;
washed out, wish-defying; so fishy
& predictable you could chart it
on a graph. What waters were you
treading when you realized no man could
write your epitaph? What Chicago,
what Sicily possessed you at that point?

DRAWING

for Elaine Ginsberg

You get right down into the physical world
when you draw; it's almost like a shoot-out
(if you want to get real & western about it).
Object & objective become one, like the gun
you pull on your willing or unsuspecting subject.
What you get is what you see; a likeness
quite unlike the idea of your target the mind
dictates when you start spraying & laying lead.
Pursuer becomes the pursued & lasooer becomes
the lasoo'd so swiftly your heart, like the sun,
sinks or must swim on the ripe horizon of love.
Everybody's beautiful when you get right down

to sketching or drawing them just as they are.
Everything is infinitely as complex as a star
at least — the east, west, north or south
of any breast, any shape, any foot, any mouth.
Nothing is the same as anything else, & yet
there's a sameness about indicating the roundness
of cellular tissue that equally applies to faces;
the faces of rock or sea or mountains or moons.

ETERNITY

I love the quiet, hard
to reach hours where
space & time yawn at you
from one galaxy to the next;
those seemingly desolate hours
where there's room to stretch
& no car horn bleating or
anybody needing you on the horn.

There are hours that feel; right
hours that push the body around
& around with buzzard authority,
that circle the death of your
energy before zeroing in to pick
on it, operating purely
by carrion clock bits & bypieces
of industrial time. And there are
trials & mistrials of hours;
the bringing of law & order
to frontier boom towns of the mind
where minutes flow like Saturday night
whiskey & seconds tick
like chorus line saloon legs
kicking in time; ticking off
the surly, macho duelers at dawn.

And then there's the rolling sea of time
whose every bubble is less than
an instant in the longest minute
God ever held anything in mind.

LEAVING HOME FOR HOME

Seattle's still behind me now, and yet
through the rain and clouds up ahead
I can make out the beginnings
of a Portland as visually improbable
as a night in Tunisia; slow, sloshing
mirage of a place kept wet and green
for a motor-footed runner like me
to come upon and see. It's somebody's
Jerusalem if not exactly mine. Me?
I'm determined to make it into Salem
then Eugene by a quarter to nine.
What's all this endless driving about?
Tell me, Ray Carver, this is your country,
your early gin of origins. So once
again, what's in Alaska? What is it about
Vancouver, Bellevue, Siskiyou, Bremerton
I'm beginning to feel? Or is that all
up to me to figure out on the fly?
And say, Lawson Inada, jazz poet of Ashland,
Oregon! You too live in this stratosphere.
What's all this about salmon and chips,
alderwood, the Cascades, bumbershoots,
Puget Sound and Mt. Rainier, green bridges,
Green Death, ale, Mt. Shasta, water, water?

Old, eternally dislocated and hungry, hugger
of earth that I am, I love it all. I love
the breezy wide-openness of Northwest

Passages; woody, wet hermetic passages,
brash and brassy with reed; axes chopping
the region smooth. Rejoicing, realizing
you don't go on being a slumbering lumberman
if you can't seed the forest for the trees.
Finally housing gets to be so high
the timber market sinks to legendary lows.
But it's this legend, it's those lows
that brought me up to this part of the world.
But where will these gullies carry me?
Where am I headed on my way back
to a California I've never seen before?
And why am I trembling at the wheel?

Even though I know the car's still
moving, I can't imagine where it'll be
taking me. And yet oil companies grow
rich whether I drive on or pull to a halt.
Salt is what my African ancestors
used to throw over their shoulders
to stop bad luck, but for me right now,
keen on gasoline and the idea of forward movement
toward a spot where there'll be
ice cream, a fire and warmth, it's this
life at the top of the map that freezes.

THE MIDNIGHT SPECIAL REVISITED

Mean old murderous Leadbelly,
Sugarland bound as sure as you're born,
no longer buzzard lopes down Fannin Street
with hat, tin can & razor in hand
in the company of another Jeffersonian,
the one known to blues hounds, white cops
& redlight sisters as Blind Lemon.

It was them yella women who finally ran
the two of them outta Houston, they say,
& it was over that long overdue long green.

Fannin Street acts like a boulevard now;
skimpy skyscrapers, condos & hospitals
& banks shadow its haunted, motorized length.
Sugarland's no longer a catch-all prison;
it's a high security suburb now, housing
a brand new kind of convict: the managerial
elite with some pro athletes thrown in.
Neither Negro nor Jew nor White Folks sing
or gather in its streets to celebrate
or do much of anything except meet the Metro.
Besides, there is no town downtown
beyond rush hour. Only Montrose boasts
of Street People & the crime rate there
is closely watched. Seriously, you'd
have to hot tail it all the way back to when
gasoline was 15 cents a gallon to find
so much as a watermelon man or a hot tamale man
or a strolling spasm band on Fannin Street.
Even the hustling gals work out of XXX'd up
stucco nudie joints now, like the one next
door to the nursery school you bike past.
But the KKK is still alive & thriving.
Christian born-againers still burn
& the fervor of their flaming return
to fundamentals crisscrosses the topless
pistol shot nights & crackles the way
lightning always splinters God's Country
— with Texan Amurican splendor.
Religious, political or not, the cops'll
still gitcha if you don't watch out!
They catch you acting too colored or
not colored enough — it's blam!
You better not stagger & you better not fight
'cause the only Miss Rosie you're liable
to see won't be coming to bail nobody

outta nowhere. As a matter of fact,
chances are the umbrella on her shoulder
& that piece of paper in her hand
will only mean she's doubling as Weather
& Anchor person tonight on the Six O'Clock News.

22 Moon Poems
(1984–1985)

ABOUT THE 22 MOON POEMS

Composed spontaneously between September of 1984 and February of 1985, while I was adrift in Italy, Yugoslavia, New York and California, these moon-inspired poems, moans and so-liloquies continue to amaze me. They are largely culled from a notebook I kept during that wistful period, when the moon — sometimes visible, sometimes not — became my confessor, companion and comforter.

My abiding affection for the moon, its beauty, its presence and magic is still as wondrous to me as it was when I used sit on the back porch steps summers in the rural Mississippi night and marvel at how moonlight could soften and brighten my atti-tudes toward those very corn and cotton fields we kids would have to be out working in once the sun began making its rounds. In those nights, I'd have secret little boy chats with the man in the moon, smug in the knowledge — gathered from ac-tive living and looking and from losing myself in science fiction — that our little green planet was only one of countless tril-lions suspended in space with no strings attached, no visible ones at least. One look at the heavens, all jammed up and crammed with stars and oceans of light and black no-light, and I knew there was something altogether marvelous about our even being here that we'd forgotten somehow or never knew about.

As that mid-Eighties summer went falling into winter, while I was on the go abroad, and later in Manhattan, San Francisco and along the Coast Highway between Santa Cruz and Half Moon Bay, I felt continuously attuned to the moon and its moods.

"You were ten thousand miles high," photographer Robert Turney told me when I bundled up and flew off to Michigan to give some readings there. He and his wife, poet Diane Wakoski, and the Paris-based American poet Susan Ludvigson had all too briefly been gig and travel mates of mine during that pre-miere visit to Eastern Europe. We were guests of the Yugoslav Writers Union on short-term Fulbright Fellowships. By the time I turned up in Dear Old Beograd to begin my busy stay, Robert, Diane and Susan were winding down. But our paths crossed bloomingly before we soared in different directions back off into the blue.

"You were so up!" said Robert. "We loved just being around you."

"I was in love with everything then," I told them while we looked at slides and prints he'd taken in Yugoslavia.

It's true that, after tunneling through several dark seasons of personal tragedy and heartbreak, I had finally begun to see some light and lightning break quietly over the Adriatic and all along the Danube. And I was in love with rivers, with the violet sea, with big skies, the mountains, golden-skinned paprika, garlic, folk churches and mosques; in love all over again with poetry and song, with plaintive elegance and simplicity of the national dance called *kolo*; in love again with both the Latin alphabet and the Cyrillic alphabet, which I'd learned a quarter of a century earlier in Russian classes at college. And because it was with life itself that I'd fallen in love, my deeply felt outlook opened me up to practically everyone I met — Serbs, Croats, Slovenes, Macedonians, Montenegrins, ethnic Albanians and visitors from other parts of the world — as I traveled by bus and by plane, by motor car, by taxi and inevitably by foot across that alluring nation, more or less the size of Wyoming, but unutterably more complex.

The rhapsodic swell of utterance that textures and colors these poems probably doesn't owe so much to the poet in me as it does to an ineluctable indwelling spirit, reachable in each of us, that emerges from its hiding place once it senses the time is right. At all times, I swear, our seemingly mute and moveable moon knew precisely where I was coming from and would have to go, while it played walkie-talkie with me. And, from my cramped human perspective, I was beginning to grasp and adore the Serbo-Croatian proverb that goes: *This century is like snow.*

— A.Y.

HERE IN VIOLET LIGHT

Here in violet light
streaming up out of the Adriatic
like the mushroomed hairdo
of some atomic façade
they're locking up the town.

Cats are curled in doorways
for the night, snoring or meowing
in Italian, & the gardens
here in Via Fratti seem relaxed
enough to want to drink
more than a little moonlight
with their water, their dew;
the dutiful need of plants
& grass & trees to soak
& stare. Hey, peeping moon!
I know you aren't about
to sing or even whisper
in the sprightly dead of this night.
In fact, the detached look of you
is far from being the jolly
fat moon that lit the riverbank
we slept on in August a month ago
when the whole flow & splash
& feel of you was the color
of the Tuolumne. You hung out
over our sleeping bags &, like
the stars, drifted off & away
in other directions (or is there
only one?) until shooting stars
took the show. That was
you, wasn't it, moon?
This Italy I'm in clouds
my mirror sometimes;
I'm not always sure
what it is I'm seeing.

Sometimes I think you're really me.
Other times I think you're the type
who'd follow me all the way
from California to Italy actually
just to see if I can keep
passing you off as a pal.

Ciao, il mio amore. Goodnight, moon.
I'll get you in my dreams.

THE TUTTI COLORI QUALITY OF LIGHT

Oooo, moon, you look so lovely
this evening floating over the shops
& facing the beach at Forte dei Marmi
as if this were just your usual gig,
no big thing; you know, just checking
everything out to make sure
the beautiful girls are still girls
& the handsome boys are still
handsome. I saw you follow
me up that main street with the old postcard
stands & toy shops & sweater boutiques
& art galleries & posh toy stores &
gelaterias; places where Forte dei Marmi
merchants get the jump on Viareggio's
who want the bigtime, spendthrift tourists
to drift their way, but who aren't willing
to get up off a lira & all the time
it takes to set it up shopping center style,
like in all the United States of Americas.

Yes, but, moon, you know as well as I do
it's the tutti colori quality of light
that eases its way into human eyes, so softly

this could be the 15th Century for all we care.
And you of course help make it that light;
you circle us that way, all smooth & bright
& darkly for effect. When the sun lends you
enough rays to spread around to make
your good impression stick & last, you zoom.
In Italy, that ain't all that hard;
all you gotta do is show up, dress the part
& the role simply plays itself.

SO IS THERE LIFE ON YOU, MOON?

So is there life on you, moon?
Some mystics say yes & most
scientists say no. What do
you say, moon of moons?
Is there any life on you?

How about inside those rocks
of yours? Are you sure
there isn't some microscopic
form of mini-seeded life-
in-embryo embedded or pillowed
in the dandruff you harbor
by all your dead & tranquil seas?

It's fun to talk about, all this,
but academic, you must admit.
I look at you & know you're partly me.
For now, that's life enough.

IN A TWINKLING, THE GREEN

In a twinkling, the green
of this Belgrade backstreet hotel window
burns impressions on my world-weary eyes
in colors that dazzle but only because
the reds & blues & aquamarines
of the pantyhose the young women wear
seems so alive in the midst of all this gray,
solid officialdom of unmuted light.
I watch the old women hanging out wash
to dry in late morning sunlight about to turn
shadowy in the September that can only become
another October, my month of solitudinous love.
Lost like this, in another world,
I grab at anything, any language to make
myself understood by these beautiful people
whom a taxi driver told me this afternoon
are, like the languages they speak,
so unsimple, maybe complicated. There is
the small electrical power plant to my left
as I lean like moonlight, my head out the window
to listen to traffic in Slavic. But
there is also further left the uphill grind
of traffic & waiting bus stop citizens who,
when the dark green & dusty silver-topped bus
arrives, will suddenly become paying passengers
clutching their sweaty dinars & waiting,
always waiting for the right stop to pop
or drop them into another curve or sudden swerve
of this moving moment; this endless now
that is forever becoming something else again.
The peasant woman in a pink dress who smokes
& smokes like all Yugoslavs everywhere
seems to be watching me from a block away.
We're really each other &, as she leans
on the backs of her legs & huffs & puffs,
I can indeed see myself in her: a sultry Slav,

a Balkan with that Asian-Mediterranean primal
    pigmentation
defining me for centuries to come. All this
& a sudden folksong duet as well, floating
up from the street momentarily in living color.

BELGRADE MOON

Belgrade moon, where are you
now that I need you?
I come into this town by way of Pisa,
by way of Milano, by way of Zagreb
& all I run into are hustlers.
A rose by any other name may be
just as sweet, but so is a hustler
to the smell: taxi drivers, hotel managers,
bellboys, pariah of the tourist trade.

Fifty bucks a night it's costing me
to put up at the Hotel Jugoslavija
in Bulevar Revolucije (revolution,
my ass!) & they treat me like
the exploitative, privileged enemy
I'm not & never was — & all in
the name of socialism.

Maybe the doctrinaire Italian Communists
are correct when they call Yugoslav communism
    il socialismo borghese, middleclass socialism.
The earthy part of me already knows this
is probably as true as the sky of more than
    billowing clouds
hanging all around this city's airport
    which I'm obliged to see circularly.
All the loves of my tiny life hang in those clouds;

loves I don't even know well yet: the flash
& gauzed-over flesh of love; the quintessential
      slivovic of love, the basic thing;
the God-is-living-my-life-with-me gulp of love.

I know no other way to put it,
this notebooked love, this recognition.
Wristwatch time doesn't quite get it.
I'm talking about a land of tremendous beauty
      where Slavic essence is me.

You got that, moon? You understand where
      I'm coming from?
Where were you when I needed you to explain
      why I had so much trouble
trying to push myself into a tomorrow
      I'm just now experiencing today?

Green pastures, uncertain skies, I love you,
      come rain or shining moon.

MOON OF NO RETURN

Moon of no return, never the same,
got you on like a silver shawl
making the train whistle squeal
Yma Sumac hitting all her ranges
at once in the white flash of night.

I love you, moon, more than mere
sea light or the fuzzy feel of clouds
rippling playfully like whiskers
across your unshaven 5 o'clock
shadow of a face, nicked & bumped
clean into the 21st Century.

I know nothing ever turns back
into what it used to be except
the soul dissolving into pure spirit.

This light, this light, light is.

WHERE THE DANUBE AND SAVA RIVERS MEET

Heartbreak October moon of sun
dying over the Danube; orange
strip of rippling light
mixed with oil of memory on water
flowing in Saturday blue confluence
where the Sava and Danube Rivers meet
I sigh at you & greet your sulking plenitude.

Why do you have to go & leave me
in this confusing desert of light?

MOON, HOW DO I MEASURE UP?

And, moon, the darkness you float in
comes and goes like light nourishing itself.
There aren't many corners left to turn
before the blaze of day begins to blossom
in the dark like a burst of colored daylight
spiraling; a flower in its black-holed center.
There's hardly room left to breathe, much less
turn & burn in the lunacy of space.
You feed me lightless dreams that roam
my bones & inner cities & come out real,

not remembered like a movie in the sky
of one eye. You watch & see me through my phases,
too cool to call me on my wrongs,
only my night which, like your nights,
is it, moon, tell me, how do I measure up?

SEE, SEE, MOON

See, see, moon, O see what you done done
(or is it done did?) I don't know
the right way to talk to you no more,
nor do I care that you don't answer me.
I've walked into rooms, their windows
overflowed with light & fresh air
& understood how big plugs of skylessness
can get translated into versions of illusion;
blinded beauty in all its fullness.

▼   ▼   ▼

But when the blues overtakes you,
every little once in a while,
bluegummed moon, all explanations fail
it seems, but no, the blues
by any other name would be
just as funky.
Why should it be so difficult
to pin the color of your sorrow

COASTAL MOON

Moon of moon & quintessential moonness,
I wonder who you are up there, quiescent,
snug & cozy in a holding pattern
vaguely reminiscent of the calm
& calming sea. And like staring
at the ocean or at fire, the wave
& flame of what I am is what I see.

I see you winking, moon, nestled
over the ocean at just about where
2 o'clock would be if the heavens
    had clock hands,
snuggled in a furry triangle of clouds;
smiling as if to whisper: "Crisper
nights have swept thru Dubrovnik."

But it's the palm-rustling wind
& softening rain that's blowing me
away & away, so completely away
I shudder to think how far
I'd have to walk if thoughts didn't have wings.

O fly me back into the light that beams
from the center of the heart of darkness.
Peel me away, moon, layer after layer;
let me shed all artifice like an artichoke
does petals until there's nothing left
except the indivisible & invisible essence:
the wondrous, disappearing joy you are to me tonight
while we play hide & seek beyond the evening.
No London bookmaker would dare lay odds
on when or where you're apt to pop up next.
And not even a seasoned Dubliner could toast
    or host you righteously.
All the same, *au claire de la lune*
(if you'll excuse my French),
in the clear & present safety of your light,

I make my way home by sullen taxi
from the wharf of rain & sea-washed stone
& stray cats with their kittens
advancing into Sunday-kept moments that grow
    newer & brighter by the minute.

Undress me to my soul, resort town moon,
& gently lay me down to sleep like you
on a bed of shiny, dark water with gypsy clouds
for cover. *Laku noč, bonne nuit, guten nacht,*
buona notte, goodnight-goodnight-wherever-you-are!

BIG OCEAN-WAVING, WOMAN-PULLING MOON

Big ocean-waving, woman-pulling moon,
I checked you out when I checked
into this grand hotel, for you were
hurrying October along, my month
of months. And there was something
about the way you took Dubrovnik
that made me want to curl up
in the midst of all this 6th Century splendor
on a bed in a single room with balcony
hanging over the endless, wayward sea
& cling to the formless source of my power,
cling to God from which all beauty flows.

You've seen it all, moon, haven't you?
But have you ever shivered in your rounds
to see how perfectly magnetic loveliness
born of flowing love can be? I have.
I have reason to believe that even
bumps on the head unhinged in a dream
can be gifts or sudden messages

delivered in blood when, from across
an uncrowded room, enchantment looms.

Here in the heart of coastal Yugoslavia
where German is germane to commerce
& English second-guessed, I drink
warm toasts to you, my wine butter-colored
& chilled in sea air. *Und das Meer*
ist blau, so blau, und das Meer ist blau.
The sea so blue, the wavelength of jeweled
    turquoise,
rings like a bell, like bone, like
familiarity itself, the common,
sacred feeling of having once known
such sumptuousness of nature —
spirit captured in sea, stone & hill
or in the green, heated light of seaside
    resourcefulness.

Overhanging, overwhelming, overcoming moon,
the birds I hear singing at 2 a.m.
in the dog-bark lushness of sweet,
chic Dubrovnik is raindrop to the cheek
to my Mediterranean soul. The palms
of my hands may be sweating from the stomach-
curdling mussels I must be allergic to
in Old Town, Stari Grad, but you comfort me
& make possible this speedy recovery
that's tugged me from the throes of throwing up
    my hands
at the heaven nestled all around me now.

PIDGIN MOON

Side 1

Moon, moon, me go now but
me no got no place go now,
so where you be? Little moon
fly outta big moon day tonight.
Is cloud is white, is cloud
is gray, is blue no go blue
black sun whisper in your face
the hot in speak like
don't speak no English.
Is light, but light no bright.
Drink strong sun, make moon.
Bump, foot go boom-boom
in night. No bomb, but bump.
Is bomb make people eat-um light;
some say bump make moon moon.
More moon, more me.
Moon, me too go now.

Side 2

Is blue the sea, is blue
the eye of moon to shine;
is blue too the way you feel
inside like sky the top of you
under the skin & red the you
give me big scare. Is red
the blood, is red the root,
is black the hair. Me feel
she no look good; got
one bad eye & see moon bloom.
Is flop in flower she bad eye;
is red the talk, is blue the heart.
Is nowhere sea but eye tell all

& sky go over moon-in-dark.
Is blue the sea, is blue
the eye of moon to shine.

SARAJEVO MOON

Come out, come out, wherever you are! Sarajevo moon, you
can't fool me. You're the same tall, full-faced joker I was woozy
with a month ago when we both blew into Yugoslavia. It hasn't
all been blues, has it, pal? We've been in some small towns and
we've heard us some small talk, but what a time it's been!
And to think you're shining tonight on the very spot where
Archduke Ferdinand of Austria got shot and — according to
simpleminded history teachers — started World War I. Do you
really think that was what started the war to end all wars? And
if not, then what, cooling moon?

SARAJEVO MOONLIGHT

Looking over my shoulder at you this morning, I'm listening to
the tender baritone voice of Radovan Karadzic in the little
Church of St. Michael the Apostle. Radovan is telling us what
a sweet, lovable place this family church of his is, and how the
light of history has shone on it twice. He narrates how St.
Michael's was burned to the ground and how, with the Sultan's
permission, it was rebuilt. The catch was that it couldn't exceed
its previous breadth or height. The heights of nights I measure
by your presence are incalculable, a gift of light so precious that
the only way to weigh it would be to shine on the scales of the
fishes in the sea. The deepening blueness of your eyes in this
Islamicized town of such cold weather breathes a frosty ring
around my icy view of you.

Walking along Saraci Street, past the bridge & the great
Yugoslav notion of divided space sliced up in slivers or
crescents or in the polyglot continuum of mountain overseen
by sea or the churning of the unseen side of all space, where
God abides & does the whole show in spare time; the play, the
acting, directing, scenery, costumes, big-Serbo-Croatian-
moon-shining-over-the-whole-stage-showcase-of-everything-
that-was-or-is-or-will-be-including-War-&-Peace-&-Trouble-
at-the-OK-Corral — all said as one word in a single sigh.

MOON OVER MATTER

Orhan Vele, Turkish listener to Istanbul, I'm cool.
When I hear your name spoken up the street from
the Ali Pasha mosque by Jasna, who teaches and studies
Muhammadan literature in Paris and all the other
right places, my blood quivers the way it used to do
when I was 15 and studied the Qur'an and went to
mosque in Detroit. But this is Sarajevo that we're
meeting in now. The magic of the Orient is rushing
in between the slats of our prayerful floor and
perfuming the walls of our thumping hearts that go
absolutely Arabic in the afternoon, especially in
the bazaar where they deal rugs and sweaters and pipes
and footwarmers and wool and yarn and old shoes and
silver and brass and, for all I know, the moon.

O don't go giving me any of your goody-two-shoes
know-how, *luna mia!* I know you got the savvy to
cover yourself once you see your cover's been blown.
I also happen to know you're hooked up with these
Turks and other Muslims, that you got hooked up
long long ago, back when sand was almost as smooth
as muslin blowing in the sour window of some
curious Bowery room curtained for all eternity and,

for all we know, like lines from a play about
friendly crow's feet tiptoeing around laughing,
browning eyes. Or the open-sesame realness of love
as it surrenders to itself, hit after hit; a torrent.

O help me out, come on, moon, would you! Hum a
few bars so I can fake it. You know enough
American to do that, don't you? I love the way
you just won't let me fly off unnoticed without
giving my wings a good going-over. I love the
sky and sea and coast and mountain and desert and
flatland of you, noon moon. Your face, your
gyrations, all the edges of your legend shushing me
with smiles of an October night — all of it a
thrill in itself.

The cooling Belgrade breeze has chilled; that chill
has iced and now we're like rubbernecked turtles
pulling back inside our shiny shells in the thinning
light darkening the Danube; the same Slavic light
of clouds reflected in the street-lit puddles around
Marx & Engels Square, or cutting through the park
to Milyosh Knez. Socialist moon, I see how hard
you hustle; how tough it is to turn a buck or stretch
a dinar these days. And it's the Slavic soul of you
that pushes me into your path, and the further I
travel it the quicker I see myself disappearing into
this body of gigantic allness, where I have always
belonged. Serb or Croat or Slovene, Bosnian Muslim,
Macedonian or Turk — it's all fast becoming a
question of moon over matter, isn't it?

MOONLESSNESS

You, you, there you go again
disappearing on me, moon,
& on the ripest of days
right smack dab in the middle
of all-autumn. No sooner
do I grow used to having you around
for days & nights on end than
the soothing shadow of you
dissolves from the heavens,
& even the taste of your light
upon the wet, shiny coat
my tongue wears in this goodbye
cartoon evaporates. Hey, loony moon!
Don't you know that even I,
a clown for love, no savvy whatever
for stately details, would gladly form
an elegant delegation of one
to swim this darkness to you?

Here in this particular now,
here where you've ditched me,
it's all these crazy, bluesy all-blues,
moon, that buoy me where I hover
at this streaky kitchen window,
soaking up the silvery orange & blue
sky across the lost green street
of redheaded October — all of it
blue, blue, ebulliently blue. This is
the now that keeps pulsing & pushing
& pulling me along this snail-like
switchback of a trail I travel moonless.

THE MOON, THE WHOLE MOON,
AND NOTHING BUT THE MOON

Glorious, nourishing, flourishing moon, swollen with
all the raw energy of time and what it does as light,
I take off my hat, my coat, my tie, my shoes and socks
to you. Breathing you in like an oceanic breeze,
how can I expect to escape the pure lure and lore of
you; the you that isn't now and never has been and
never will be the moon, the whole moon and nothing
but the moon?

Love pours from every leaky look I take of you and
all your ceilings. You're no roof, but the sky is,
and tonight's the night, you beautiful, bright streak
of wonder; particle of this particular eternity. I
give you everything I've got, which isn't much, but
all yours for the reaching, friend of light.

Little by little, *poco a poco*, I surrender. *Surrender.*
The most reassuring word in this locked-up language.
Surround me with your intelligence and strength. I
surrender, I surrender to the power of your love.
All I want to be is with you every special moment of
the day and night, waking or sleeping, on the move,
restive, or stilled in contemplation. Your powering light
and the force that sanctions it is both of us together
and a dream, alive and well and welling in the gulf-
stream of your eyes.

I give the world right back to you, my God, sweet lover
of my soul; my only life. The light that holds you up
in space keeps me afloat and shakes the limbs of trees
and men alike. Outside my window now, in loving
Socialist October, an answer comes before I've even
asked my question. And over and over it whispers
along my sunlit, autumn cheek the sobering sound: Yes,
yes, yes, yes, yes, yes. Da.

SING A SONG OF SINGAPORE

You will of course remember the night
in Singapore just before it turned yesterday,
when I walked into a McDonald's,
burnt out on West Australian &
    Southeast Asian food,
with you shining after me like
You've done for millions of years
over shy Chinese girls & boys
& their emperors & empresses.
And when the quiet Malaysian girl,
    her English as murky as rock & roll,
asked me to join her with her husband at table,
I felt funny but followed.

"You like to see our wedding pictures?"
    she asked.
An impure American, I knew & loved
    nothing more than wonder.
I wondered what new kind of come-on this was.
Her New Zealander husband, a soldier,
young like her & curious, had only wanted
to talk with another native speaker of English.
Yet there they sat with their Big Macs & stacks
of albums just picked up from a photographer's
studio up the street, their pages plastered
in ceremony with matrimonial pictures
    of their recent union;
this pair in their teens, more than 20
years younger than myself. They wanted me
to see their tux & gown, their cake, their feast
    & relatives from west & east;
it was real the feel of it that surprise.

And, moon, the wine of you was pouring
silence & effortlessness across the sky
at the center of my light-soaked life,
just before storm after storm began

to break, recede and break again.
It was all too soon to know you'd set
all this up, my dignified friend;
mile by mile, all the while waiting outside
    behind the wheel, ready to roll,
moving real slow like a Southern aunt
on a dusty road about to disappear
down another kind of black hole —
    no space.

Sing a song of Singapore,
    dance your happenstance.
But most & more & best of all,
    don't go, don't go, don't go!

THE MOON UP CLOSE IN WINTER BY TELESCOPE

1

You jump right out of your skin
by the eye of your chattering teeth
to hear the hawk talking
while the moon listens.
The yard becomes a container
for this chill of recognition;
this light, this icy light warming
the eyelidded rims of the world.

2

Standing in the night sky
suspended by a lens,
the mind zigs and zags
at possibilities, magnitudes;
the worming of light into spaces

beyond distance, brilliance
broken up into shards of God everywhere.
You can only blink, astonished again
to see how every kind of viewer
has its limits and conventions.

    3

Did D.W. Griffith really invent
the close-up, the medium shot
and the fade-out? Or did we
in our automatic dreaming
always zoom in and pull back
on windy, moon-swept nights?

THE ORCHARD AT NIGHT IN RAIN LIGHT

for Mary Laporte

From the soothing distance,
another moon,
this one unexpected,
but I'm flexible.

I can squeeze it
into my night & morning
can wait until these clouds
blow over.

       O don't you
know & love the ache
new moonlight draws
from blood unmilked for days?

Steaming as it warms

the moody last of winter
sky, this fruity light is right
on time to set heaven on fire.

WAKING UP IN SANTA CRUZ AT SEA

Over my shoulder, to the left,
the left — what's left of the moon:
a slivery-edged scoop of silver
light coming at me sideways
this morning in its happiness aspect.

And what is happiness but the secret
teachings of sorrow turned inside out,
flipped like a fallen coin landed
to stand on its in-between? *Clink!*
The sound of glass against the wash basin
I drink from. *Squish.* Soap slippery
in my hands letting go of all pasts
in this friendly new bathroom.
Being in this rented room, in this ranch-
like orchard house, with farms to smell,
and getting a last look at the old
moon is newness renewing itself.

It's morning in America, palomino moon.
I could straddle and ride you cool
across these misty Zen hills
greened over with glens and lightning
dips. We'd gallop clear down to the sea.
This global daybreak, straight
along Highway 1, your golden mane
of light streams back at me, warming
and tickling my washed, facial vision:
a horse-powered moon with no shoulder
to pull over or cry on in either direction.

CAROLINA MOON

There is no greater moon to contemplate
than you, June in January moon, refusing
to be identified or associated with endings
or beginnings or middle-aged psyches on fire
with time. Your southern extremities
burn down to San Diego, Oxnard, Taft, Mexico
and the showbiz center of it all — El Lay.

You're nothing like the Carolina moon,
Monk's dreampiece; you're no Charlotte,
no Raleigh; there ain't no tar
on your fleet heels, but you are the only
one around, the only moon I feel
we've got, and still cooling; a clumpy star.
The power that hours still need to rotate
pinwheel-style from the center to the aisle
of love: isolation from the stage we dance
and do our magic upon. I don't know why
juggling should be so tough in this spring,
in this world of firewood ventriloquists.

Sea Level
(1986–1990)

JOLT

Human love is all electrical, a whirring
of negative & positive ions, pardons & hardons.
The ginger kiss of love is baked, a snap
to finger, a mouthful to handle & silk
to the tactile mind of breathprints
& loping voltage. If there's a sky
in your eye, you can bet it's electrical,
connecting you up up up with an optic nerve
that in itself is curved with skylight.
Thus do we each & all fit together in puzzle
fashion to form one all-inclusive gap.

CITIZEN CB

Twister to Magnum
Sweet Jesus to Masterpiece
Chicken George to Brown Sugar
Use the side band, gentlemen's agreement
Are you from Mars?
I'm trying to be
He gon say we took the stitches outta his britches
Look what you started, Lone Ranger
She's trying to be his great great grandsister.
Hey, Short & Sassy!
Terrible!
You tell that redneck to watch his mama
cause she might come out one night
& find a dog on her back
Mister Ginger Bread Man'll be here
What kinda sucker is this?
Gray Pumpkin? . . . Gator Roy . . .
I like to spread bread with peanut butter
& then lick it & lick it . . .

Mister Sunjammer
A great big bundle of mistletoe to you
I'll give you a meal, enough left over
    to put in a doggybag
Fall by the ponderosa by 11, no,
    that's too late, maybe 10, yeah 10
Tar Baby moved up to Stockton —
    & that's a big 10-4
San Jose Queen with Kinky to Devil Potion
Flush your hammer down, wig out, we gone
You know somebody gonna come in there loose
    & do a job on em
Well, have a howdy doody fine one
You say you a Buddhist, you wearin boots?

FLU

for Diane Wakoski

Slow, the chill that gravitates
to the marrow of your bones
stops there and spreads in aching swirls
throughout your loggy limbs.
Your calming acupuncturist, Dr. Lee,
points out the weakening powers
of ill-tempered diet, or possibly
too much alcohol or beef or spice.
She also warns against the shock
of taking ice-cold beverages on the rocks.

You walk against December, remembering
her advice, windy in your scarf
and heavy sweater, coated like a tongue.
The sky looks watercolored, pumped
with inky grayness in a stark loose blue.

You think about the needles, then tattoos
and vaguely picture the kind of divine artist
who'd let her paintbrush bleed a paper sky.

From within you're bleeding poisons
your body tastes and knows on sight
the way it knows the feel of wellness, or
its need for the five tastes: sweet, sour,
salty, bitter and tangy. Readying yourselves
for the long rest in a slow flushing-out
of what isn't you at all, you lay your head
upon a troublesome, unreasonable pillow
and wait for dreams to lift you to their level.

Asleep, you let another you take charge;
the one that doesn't chill, nor does it warm;
that knows no slow or fast, no gravity.
Feathery as light, this you means business.
With all doubt moved clean out, miracles
are free to go to work inside the blood factory.

AFRAID

There is no fall that wouldn't break itself
if letting go became the name of the game.
Do oranges worry about falling
to the ground and splitting? Does the ocean
ever worry about being washed away
or drowning in itself? And what of borders,
margins — Georgias afraid of becoming
Alabamas? Europes or whole Americas petrified
by the specter of the Yellow Hordes; sunlit
clouds that freeze at thoughts of sunlessness?

What is it we hurt when we do bottom out
or go broke? In what darkness do the drowning
see and picture themselves looking good
while light itself appears to fall away?
What do we overlook when we're afraid?
The worst is that we'll lose our lives, we think.
But to whom is life lost? To leave-takers
or those left? We only guess at loss
and what it costs. What is there to wash away
but darkness? And who is ever left out except
the frightened? The heart that breaks still beats.

NO STRINGS ATTACHED

Beneath the grain
of every human move
you'll come upon Pinocchio
as wired with wonder &
oceanic notions & airs
as any lumbering whim
born of man alone

Yet somewhere beyond
the length of that nose
or those quivering donkey ears
you'll discover quite another
soul altogether, a smooth one
who says yes & yes & yes
to all your splintery no's

HANGOVER

The preferred pain of the Western World,
it might be crime & punishment, both,
all at once the stomach, in a sea of sickness,
wants to relieve itself of being
a part of the body, wants to travel upward
out beyond the zone where swallows live,
where simple mouthings recite the oracular.
Crime & punishment: the protestant ethic
of Christian churchkey indulgences.
Why not the effulgence of airy mornings
by the ocean? Why not a deeply breathed belief
in the easy joyfulness of surrender?
Where does it say you have to poison yourself
to have what passes for a good time
in this world of sudden spills & afternoons
crowded with longings to be drunker than drunk?

THE BEAUTY OF MILWAUKEE COLD WITH RAIN

The beauty of Milwaukee cold with rain
is warm enough to melt us *and* the snow.
Somehow the freeway sight of it seems sane.
Out here where traffic's thawed, it's stop and go.
Who says recycled lake cloud doesn't cleanse?
Your ride's saved me; my car gave up and died.
But when I see your staunch Mercedes-Benz
stuck out here too, preserved, for all its pride,
I have to laugh. And if this drizzle lasts,
we're on the skids; this snow'll turn to mush.
No chains was dumb but, *brrr*, these polar blasts
reduce the city to a whitened hush!
And rain is what our stalled Milwaukee needs;
with rain the lanes move up and bloom, like seeds.

SON

You should hammer on him to clean
his undersea room? You should stay
on his back or up in his chest
until he picks the clothes
up off the floor, unglues old gum
and fudge and snot and pizza sauce
from chairs and shelves, and drags
the mildewed bathing suit and towel
from under his bed, until he sweeps
and dusts? What for? What drawer
should you pull out to prove
your power over him? The lesson
when you were going to school back home
was this: At 13 you do your best
to let your loathesome parents know
they're not the ones who run your show.

A little well-staged chaos is in order.

THE LOVESONG OF O.O. GABUGAH

Time to split now, you & me
got things to do, got stuff to see,
like Frankenstein breakin loose from his slab
all charged up with juice & ready to swoop
right out the front door & down the stoop
past alleyways & neon signs
& people waitin in movie lines:
runs that lead like a big commotion
for all we know into the ocean
where they keep tellin us all life was born . . .
Hey, dont stand there goin, "What's happenin, Gus?"
Let's split before they start zappin us.

Up the street the girls & bitches brew
scuttlebutt about J.R. & Donahue.

The snowy line that blows its way up $100 bills,
the snowy freeze that jacks its frost off $100 bills
cornered all its licks into one big evening of tongue,
went crazy tryin to figure out its next move,
whooshed up the chimney clean, burnt out a nose,
& sniffin all there was to know about July,
just blew its ownself out, forget the rose.

BEAR GULCH ROAD

The hills of this tractor
land unspeculated moves
across itself in savory rolls
the way a redwinged blackbird
traverses her misty green hills.
Satori was never like this.
I picture you sweating
just beyond the furthest
of these California land-
clearing mounds of earth,
the grass beneath your feet
& your mind in the heaven
of hikers. Yellow tractors
of thoughts are plowing the air
around you as you look up
to see there's far more sky
than land or sea to understand.
You're walking by foot;
I do it by eye. Slowly
you reach the summit out there,
precisely at the spot
where our seeing each other

becomes the only point of arrival.
Harvest me the meaning
of the way it looks this morning.

H_2O

Not only were you waiting
for this moment to arrive;
the melted ice of what you are
is waiting in a dish to learn
its future by degrees.

You can boil that into steam
or back it into the fridge
to freeze. Either way
it's one and the same moment.

There's no way oxygen and hydrogen
won't combine again in the exact
same formula to make time
more interesting than memory.
The cloud of doubts surrounding
my own flesh is as real as
these open-hearted pines
edging the afternoon with majesty.

The wonder is this: that eternity
bothers itself at all with all this waiting,
but keeps arriving and departing
from itself; fluent, hilarious and punctual.

ROMANCE WITHOUT FINANCE

If you can't finance it undercover,
you needn't apply for the gig of lover.
To stake this whittled down version of love
you don't need money so much as time,
attention & all the me the mind can see.
Still, moments turn up with dulling precision
when the heads or tails of your nighttime
    thereness
must be flipped to recall your daytime
    awayness;
no win, no lose, just edgily the blues.
As money needs spenders & spenders need lenders,
so passionate romance seems always in need
of love, back-talk & deliberated speed.

SUMMER

Evening is the Fourth of July;
stars the sizzling fireworks
advertising the night. The moon
rolls tender-bellied toward the sun,
smoothing darkness from the beach.
The ocean bellows blues below sea level.

Giddy from the ferris wheel, I stare
down into carnival light at dawdling
hordes along the boardwalk, cooling out
in their crumpled, listless casuals,
their pastel-tinted hair a sushi
of shadow, glitter & pierced ears.

Breeze, what reckless celebration
are you hinting at? Maybe you've blown in

to singe us by the sparks of our own souls'
roman candles, or flaring cherry bombs, or
to let us see ourselves aglow in showers
of hot & flaking light.

SEA LEVEL

Even a hair
when you bend closely
to look at it on the beach
beams red & yellow & blue
& green the very way
prisms imprison light
& break it up into colors
It all seems to be
a matter of getting down
close enough to look
& see what is & what isn't

Sea level is where we
mostly don't live
yet under the cloud-bright sky
next to the endless sea
next to the endless ocean
we see on the level
& blending vision oceanic
with the shy horizon
the distances shorten
& the moments lengthen
rather after the manner
of sand that doesn't know
it's sand all by itself
but only when a billion grains
gather together in its name
Let white light flame

into every color it wishes
Just give us the power to see

SOMETIMES WITH THE WAVES

Sometimes with the waves
smacking at my feet & the sky
with its tender clouds &
almost tame blueness looking
as if it wants to get into the act,
I sense the true you awash
all around me, splendid
in your perfect invisibility;
disguised as nothing less than everything
& hence unnoticeable, undetected.
Surely that's how an ocean works —
each particle is at once a wave, yes,
or part of one, & every splash goodbye
is really a hello, no? I go crazy
just thinking about how you keep me
on my toes & head over heels in awe.

BIG SUR

after a pastel by Vivian Torrence

Sometimes it's the look of love
along a coast like Big Sur's
that galvanizes even the wash
& splash of blueness foaming
into green upon the rock &

circumstance of cliffs & promontories.
The blush of blooming seaplant,
the bloom of abalone blows even
the minds of oldtime naturalists
when the tide pours in and Indian
souls rush out to fill the night.
But always it's that look, that
luscious, lingering look rolling
in & out of cloud & wave alike,
that spills onto the leaves of fog
journals, that changes in its sameness
century on top of century, glimpsed
in a watchful, wakeful moment
along such breathable stretches
of majesty & heartbeat in the rush
of oceanic sureness on the big coast
trafficked by foot & by motorcade
with no mist to ground love down.

LIFE AT THE BACK OF THE PLANE

In a tobacco trance
they genuflect
at the elbow
to their twisting god

In hazy sacrament
pungent as lust
they blink with disregard
at up-front pilgrims
to the john & think:
"An infidel the Lord
of Tar has spared
this aching ecstasy.
Ah, better death than breath!"

If it must always begin
with the captain
turning off the no-smoking
sign then why not end
with the one-lunged traveler
the little old man on the aisle
in seat 62F who when he hears
"Please extinguish all
smoking materials,"
pushes to the floor
the blanket that's been
smoldering in his lap
and tromps upon it two-footed
while the congregation
overwhelms him with
volleys of amens & hallelujahs?

THE NEW MODE OF PRODUCTION

There were moons O there were moons
& stacks of stars revealing the night
for what it was: a batch of noons
blackened & lengthened with delight.
Night seemed to be the place to screen
vision from blindness, shadow from act;
where, in fact, the deepest green
was keeping me sane & in contact
with the rest of the world, its labor
force chopped up into little Chads
& Chinas & Singaporous Mexico neighbors
to accomodate hi-tech high-jinks & fads.
Assembly meant one thing; research another.
The idea was to promise nothing, nothing
but the idea of plant with seed as mother

FLIRT

Like somebody's ass in a Friday Nite Video,
stop-framed to rock & shock the world
out there looking, the sweet wiggle
of your thought-waves saves me hours
of guessing who's kissing me now.
Lust is just that crazy; a lazy display
of worn-out backseats. *Nowhere to run to* . . .
Nowhere to hide . . . Let's put this on rewind,
pretend the beginning's the end. Let's
pretend you'll let me think you never winked.

THE MOUNTAINS OF CALIFORNIA: PART 2

Slow-rolling beauty
without end or beginning
assures our immortality.
The way an orchid chorusing
her fragrance in waves
says no goodbye is possible
in this joyous voyage.
Nowhere do we feel the fall
more fully than in spring,
for summer is the mirror
winter warrants. Transfigured,
life masks and mocks itself,
pretending to be dead asleep,
as if it cannot help
but leaf and flower from itself.
As enchantment keeps
reaching us in looks and takes,
so the firm and melting faces
of the irreducible are always
losing their life in its love.

THE HAWK REVISITED

It's always been like this with me
in winter: no meaning to my morning
nor my moaning either if
I can't touch you unforgettably.
You like to be remembered, don't you?

What I like to do most is goose;
ask any moose about my thrust.
I wouldn't trust me in a pinch,
much less in a storm. I inch
my way into your confidence, get
under your skin and, boneward bound,
put spells on you that chill.
You like to be remembered, don't you?
When I catch you out walking
in your unlined Navy peacoat,
forgetting Ohio ain't California,
that's when I know to swoop down
& give you a fresh taste of how
it used to be when you still lived
in Michigan always under a cloud.
You still like to be remembered, don't you?

REGGIE'S VERSION

for Reginald Williams
in memory of James Baldwin

My girlfriend, you know, she
bought me this quart of beer
& a package of Doritos &
it was funny because she don't drink
no beer much. I couldn't

figure it out. Then she told me,
said: "James Baldwin died today.
Baby, I'm sorry, but I knew that'd mean
something to you. I don't know
anybody else trying to do what
you're trying to do — write."
So she brought me this beer &
I poured us both some & sat
& thought about it for a long time.
Man, I was touched; I was really moved.

FROM BOWLING GREEN

The prompt sadness of Schumann or Tchaikovsky
is the wistfulness of Basho or Bukowski
in a furnished apartment that happens
to hold me now in January-glacial splendor.
As love condenses into ice and snow
forms the steam that bleeds from molten lava,
so music and its poetry will ooze
with sweet symphonic arias and blues.
Getting used to appearing in a poem or song
means becoming comfortable with life. The long
way around usually ends up being the shortcut.

GRIZZLY PEAK

The low-burning moon of moons
heats Grizzly Peak the way
Berkeley used to build a fire
under San Francisco. One

monkey *can* stop a show &
this time it's the monkey moon
again, firm & complete; the key
to every lonely person's grief.

Relief is seeing the motion
of the yea-saying eye freeze
across skies who've known suns,
as many as 50 suns to 5 moons.
And there the mystery collapses.
Kisses take over; the simian
complex, sainthood, Hearst Castle.

Always the news is the same:
Grizzly Peak Bears All Its Beauty
Unalone, surrounded & peopled
by sightseers day & night.

IAN

after Jean Jones

If this is showbiz, then am I
getting older or colder or what?
Hitler thought he had a hit or
Mao Mao Mao Ma-Ma Uma-Mmm-Mao!

Spying on the species some nights
it's all I can do to live in
my own little world without wasting
all those prize zombies clapping

while we zap 'em one by one, two by two;
with nothing else to do, they guzzle up brew

and move. Baby, necrophilia was never
brainless like this. Some nights it's all

I can do to leave in my own little world
with no take-out windows, without weather,
without getting drawn like a moon
or a tune or some sexy wet cartoon

into their whirling world out there;
as high and dry as my glittering fly.
Take away zero from zero, you know what
you got. But nothing short of our sound

can chill this crowd — "Whooooweeee!
Damn good show!" And if we didn't have sex
in our name, it might suddenly matter
when they scream: "What you wanna play next?"

All you need to know about this show
is we're in charge, is I'm the one pouring
all the juice that keeps these wires live.
If this is showbiz, then what am I?

THE INDIANA GIG

In glassy, incandescent glory
the ascent hastens me home
all over again; a gig is a gig.
But something real & big looms here.
You can see it woven into the warp
of light & sound around the edges
of this morning. The way that dog
is woofing across the grassy lot
of dawn & up behind the sycamores.
Home was never a place to begin with,

but sly effulgence that keeps
leaking & looking out from nowhere.

Sometimes you sound it as "Back Home
in Indiana," other times it's Miles'
"Donna Lee," but always, always
there's a Hoosier drowsiness
spread in lazy splendor out across
the soul's industrial, farmed-out heartland.
To catch it completely, it's sometimes
necessary to drop down an octave,
hear it as being downsouth, only breezier,
& the flight's almost complete.
You're ready to turn as red as any leaf
in the Indiana summer of playful lemonade,
axle grease, corn & tractored slow ball.

Uncollected Poems
(1956–1990)

PRELUDE

for Roland Navarro

What is nightfall
In that dismal land?
Or the quaint lull
of Sunday finding its end?

His favorite reading
Was that of spring light,
And of hard fighting,
And of painted feet.

Could they have known
They would have prayed
At some gilded throne
While he sullenly toyed,

Bewitched his tending aunt,
Patted dry wept blood,
Prepared anew for the hunt.
At best he's softly praised.

April, 1956

IN THE TENDER WOODLAND

In the tender woodland
where peace drips like cool rain
from the silence-drenched leaves
of poplar trees at twilight,
I stand upon a cabbage-clean rock
and look toward the gray pines,
where moonlight has tangled itself.

1958

THE BITTER SPRING AGAIN

for B.

Hands and arms and legs and mouths
Rippling in a fluid, lapping motion
Cannot be yours in the embryo of love,
For you are motionless in this way;
Stillborn, like a stone asleep;
Not dead — asleep, like a stone asleep.

In the winter of hoping,
In the spring of remembering,
You have dragged through life
Bubbling like a seltzer,
Decaying like a fallen leaf;
Constructing triangles in rivers,
Crushing caresses in the head.

1959

OLD WOMAN

In the warm mud of alcoholic gloom
You wallow, sinking deeper and deeper
Into the substance of your undoing.
How many tears rusted that smile?
How many nights got lost in that dark face
Decaying with the gentle futility
Of living a lie, an enormous lie?
Had you a soul, it would be of stone;
To touch it would icen the hand.
But you dont have a soul. No —
The drinks washed that away, old woman;
The drinks, the enormous lie, and love.

1959

ELECTION NIGHT POME

What more is there to say in a pome?
I ask that each time I sit to write.
Past 21, Ive said a helluva lot of it.
Sitting at my desk, swallowed in sorrow,
I see Venus steaming in the western sky.
I review my Marx, come up with the same vow.
There's an evil in this land that hovers
Far beyond the economic slums of my childhood.
I walk through the rained-out night and go
To see Alain snuggled close to his beloved
In the living room of their dinnertime house.
He's aloof, philosophical about life, he's French.
I share my beer with them and watch the flame
That rises in their eyes when they look at
Each other in the smoky room — joyousness!
He's lucky — in love whether with woman or not.

I admire him for that & drink to them both.
On the TV set, I watch the election results
That come rolling in like a chain letter —
More and more each time, Kennedy leading.
I have never cared much for the body politic.
I remember the promise of plenty when
There's hunger midst plenty & I remember the
Promise of never-a-man-betrayed-to-man.
And I grow weary of the world as statistics.
Wandering back home, I remember Man
And think of the paper that's due I havent done
And Venus alive in the west & I hold
My breath and decide it doesnt really matter who
Wins just so I can preach the brilliance of
The body humanity and get a good night's sleep
Like Alain, with or without woman.

1960

BERKELEY POME

O San Francisco lighting the truth of
That olde chestnut, what was it? —
To love is not to know someone
Something anything no-thing —
Over the Oakland Bay Bridge bright
With oceaned light to the likes
Of that hilly wee Berkeley town
Of the beetle-battle, the bottled battle,
Where, unblushing, I behold
Sally in her cage, blonde and blue;
Charlie in Limbo, blue-brown;
Arline in the air, dark and darkening;
Love writhing in its cage,
Its air-heavened Limbo unlit but

Darkening, brightening, what's the name?
San Francisco, Saint Francis? —
You? the same man who scared them all
With your love of any- and no-thing?
I flutter inside like a eucalyptus leaf
Bell-blown up near Campanile Tower.

1961

SELF-PORTRAIT: HOLDING ON

Sitting in the kitchen
of a strange room
surrounded by fixtures
a window on my left
window on my right
the slow pouring of light
into the room
into my head
filled with old wine
the whole outdoors is ticking
inside I feel as black as distant trees
in the dead of night
there's nowhere to go
nothing to do
I bolt for the door
take to the streets
down several pitchers of beer
paint endless pictures of contentment
while picking warm guitars
munching bad food
holding in my head
cold hands to my hotheadedness.

1961

LESSON

That early training
sure will get it

My ma would bop me
right on the head
any time she caught me
bent over the sink
drinking water
out the faucet

Now I do it every time
always remembering
her mindful slap,
the lovingness

1963

ARE YOU THE LOVER OR LOVED?

Well, are you the lover or loved?
the caresser or caressed?
the undresser the undressed?

They say the lover loves
& the beloved is loved
but I say neither is either,
for only either you are neither

1963

MADRID 1963: SOME CHANGES

Cin Cin Cin Cinzaaaano, pow
hands up señor it is end of the world

    Yes it's me & I'm drunk again
up inside greasy spoons off the Gran Via
having survived evolutionary sadness
for wine with my fish & TV commercials

        ▼   ▼   ▼

Voyages, ahoy —

    O my past tensions:
disguised as the Wolf Man I'll never get a haircut

        ▼   ▼   ▼

Edinburgh gals at American Express
    giggly concern for my mailishness.
    I shd quote them Annie McIntosh
    on Scotland where she sez:
    "Land of Cold Knees" circa 1960 A.D.

        ▼   ▼   ▼

Me African friends at Café No Recuerdo
    wasted on Plato, Franco's colonial pilots,
        theyd tell me where to go,
           they drink me beer toasts
           honor of my blood
    (as if theyd heard its lonely gurgle)

        ▼   ▼   ▼

Little Cuban lady (also Afro-)
    requires an Extra who can sing
        for a *colour* movie she's shooting

concerns spooks in Spain
(That aulde Scot song do go:
    "Boots of spanish leather" — O dont it?)

▼ ▼ ▼

I am simply a drowsy young moor
    straight out of Ecclesiastes
        vanity vanishing
            at a dollar a day,

                          Olé.

                                1963

DAY KENNEDY DIED

Morning of sleeplessness up to heckle wife as jokes
    are in order, relax on the mattress looking at
    Braque pictures in a book but uneasy because I
    have trouble looking at some of them

Flash into oldtime mind state CONFUSION grow drowsy
    & dream sex to bed to bed in my sleep a slow
    dream in tight squeaky balloons of clear light
    & color hours pass this way then she busts in
    to the room at 4 pm with the news

JFK's been shot thru the head in Dallas Texas & up
    I jump to tell somebody else pass it on —
    Linda upstairs in front of the TV says "O that's
    old news I been watching it since 11:30 & they
    already carried his body from Dallas to Washington
    & they already swore the other guy in" —

During speculation about Oswald's guilt Clyde & Vert
      drop in for dinner of ham then Perry Jan & Kenny
      at night but I got to sing songs at the Cabale
      so sing DEATH DONT HAVE NO MERCY IN THIS LAND
      — Rev. Gary Davis — of soft spirits pleased with
      bass player & guitarist alike but every boy &
      female's sad

Later a little wasted on vodka back home & a joint we
      fall asleep in unknown front-room darkness of
      red panties, stockings, dirty briefs & butts,
      all (but for the sound of these words) dead

                                          1963

MALCOLM'S MESSAGE

There is great peace to be earned
learned reluctantly
because as planet
we are truly nowhere

My own ignorance: the bid for love
thru ego
recognition
must go
(the actual lies I have lived hurting
to cherish)

We are one species addicted in darkness
to odious habits

[291]

that destroy us
by the half-life

Poets & all who re-present the Power
of ineffable Spirit
must draw back curtains
to show us
the beautiful stages
to which we're to ascend
where Soul continues
in revelation of
its true self
freed

Mind is greater than all matter,
Love greater than all that matters
all Creation bears witness as
out of all the vast notions
in the all-containing space of mind
we rehearse
cinematically
the doing
away
of one brother
by
another
by
assassination

1964

TINY SELF-PORTRAIT

My body & my self
joined here in this moment
rejoicing in the wind
music on the wind
body inhaling/exhaling
self cluttered in body

1963

THELONIOUS: AN INTRO

Now is the time to
listen to Thelonious Monk
a man who
for more years
than many of us
have been alive
has been making his bid
for recognition
not only among
the jazz cognoscenti
but also among
laboring men & women
of our glorious fatherlands
& motherlands
a man who has been
for free enterprise
what Kenneth Patchen
was for the detective novel
a man whose patience
a man whose endurance
is winning for him
a place in the hearts

of all good earthlings
be they black
be they white
be they yellow
or be they brown
we now proudly present
"the high priest of bebop"
Thelonious Sphere Monk

1964

O!

Alone again but happeeee
I'd give anything to stay this way

My ma on the telephone says
"Let it all go Al let it go"

She means turn it loose
whatever it is got you tied
for in the end youll have to wait anyway

1964

ROMANCE

This is not to be acknowledged thru usual channels,
        I am to be forgiven
            all
            the
               time,

you dont know these lemontrees
      the way I do. You dont know
this particular lemontree that fell me,
in love with itself
          the spring of 1964,
Arl & I we were at Gary's little house
        in Delaware St
      the clock was tocking Youth
         with a wet smile to send you
            on yr way

Ah Arl
      Ah Gary
           Ah, the lil house in Delaware St
            Ah, my lemontree its fruit
      its green goosepimply skin
         in the round, the God flesh,
we spied one another thru backyard leaves,
      all my mind went straight back
        into that cool inner sun,
we walked to Today's Market 3 abreast
      under lavender sky
        toy tinkle stars
to bus stop applause of teenagers,
walked right into that market,
      sillier than naughty
          &
      almost there
         among the Fresh Produce
   dissolved.

                1964

WHAT HAVE YOU GOT OF YOUR OWN

What have you got of your own
(raining here as I write this)

What would it be like to own rain,
great streaks of water fall
from the sky wetting every thing
on this earth needs watering?

Could you lease it out at, say,
ten dollars the inch per homeowner
roughly compounded semiannually

Nah, how vain to own rain —
better to own the TV dinner or TV,
the meal you can gobble alone
but the set's another thing,
beware the discredit bureaus:
"Lookit you owe us fifty bucks
& we didnt even ask for your business"

You dont even own your own heart
nor love nor speech nor body

You dont even own your own self
for that's imprisoned in ego
I go you go every damnbody goes

1964

THE MOUNTAINS OF CALIFORNIA: PART 1

These demonstrations of the one God,
green in the springtime in wintertime too
& all that time John Muir was out here
             living with them,
breaking himself in on them,
I just ride amongst them inside a car,
flip the radio off out of respect
& out of the feeling that there are
             more important waves
floating in & out of us, mostly thru us

The mountains of California,
do I have to say anything?
I love all this evidence
set up to surround me this way,
mountain, ocean, you just name it

                               1964

NO MORE DOORS TONIGHT

We dont drive so long distances are out
but we did take a taxi cost $2.40
all the way up to Chabot Rd
to sleep in the Pattersons' backyard
comes complete with creek & stars
— Orion for instance —
Cold
blankets
on top of
blankets
SEE
& in the morning

birds
ferns
ground
sun
keeps us dumbfounded
past noon
unthinking of
creature love
which we perform gratis
in California yet

1964

HALLUCINOGENIC HALLELUUUU

Who is director of this movie
called Cosmos
with or without
stage prop
chemicals,

sweet drugs
taken to confirm
basic
human
lonelinesses,

taken to relieve
a longing
drugstore theater
can-
not
cure
?

1965

KOTO MUSIC/SINGING

Out of silence

     sound

The emptiest landscape
     rolls into
         proper flower

All alone
    the blank heart
       sprouts by surprise
        sighs

      float up

       to

      silence

                    1965

YOU DON'T KNOW WHAT LOVE IS

in memory of Eric Dolphy

Another of my new black angels
        is singing
& even now his restlessness
        is murdering me too

The tape recorder dares to sing back
        old yearnings faithfully
as I attempt a new walk on out
        into heaven
trembling, faked out by my own shadow

                                        1965

THE RUNDOWN AT NED'S BAR B.Q.

for Ward & Mary

No unh-unh no hot sauce for me

1944 when I was ballin a truck
    outta L.A. up here into Oakland
        I stopped in one nite this little jump-up joint
            & ordered me up some ribs & french fries
                & it was a bottle settin there on the counter
            I dont remember what the name of it was
        but it had a devil on it I do know that

    so I commence to dashin that mess
all upside my little somethin to eat
    & dug on in jim I dont play with no food
        I mean I was chompin down like a champ

so long afterwhile that stuff had me sweatin
like I'd been totin a ton & a half
on my back clean thru a steambath
& my butt got to itchin & I'm up there scratchin
& drankin up pop tryna cool down some

till just about the time I pulled into town
I had to stop off & take me a cold-ass shower
& I aint jivin I was still on fire

so then I mean what the outcome of it was
& you can ask my old lady if you think I'm lyin
man I ended up they had to operate on me
I was laid up for weeks behind that devilish sauce
or whatever the hell it was
you won't catch me foolin with it no more

1965

NO TRESPASSING

for Wardess Taylor

Tuesdays all his kids would be out
like a light, one-two-three, and
their mother too, set loose in dreams
like a feathery pent-up goose

You'd drop by his place where he'd rub
his jaw in the candlelit dining room,
sip from his ale and pour you some
(Green Death they called it), and you could
barely hear his voice above Miles' *Kind of*
Blue whisper: a muted sonance so tranquil
that he'd named his firstborn son Miles too

"Sorry, man," he'd say, "if I don't do
much talking tonight," and how could you mind?
"It's my one free night to get back
next to myself, you know?"

                    Yes, you knew,
and that was the whole idea (if there was
an idea) — You'd only entered his home,
but he'd entered the music, safely, his mansion.

                                        1965

DREAMS OF PARADISE

Ive had dreams of Paradise where all you do is open your heart
& let the endlessness ooze out. It is quite something to go thru.
One night in Detroit — the death of my stepfather — weary &
hopeful of everything, I lay in bed grieving & wondering,
whereupon, 4 in the morn, the whole room began to expand &
I with it, giddy with silent affirmation — that is to say: It was
the feeling I feel each of us is rightfully entitled to & it doesnt
happen out in the world of gold & crashings but is a perfect
withinness, a peacefulness & surprise that is unkillable

                                        1965

BLUES IN DECEMBER

Wasting money & running to the store,
seem like aint nothin worth it no more —
Brew & turkey & sweet potato pie
How many years before I die?

Sit to rest & go on the nod,
shameful now in the eyes of God —
Weary & forgotten I'm scared I'll flip
If I don't take off on some trip

1965

NEW MOON OVER GROVE STREET

I'm just happy to be being
an insect recipient
of sweet rich light
cutting as it do
straight thru night
relieving chimneys
television aerials
in the vicinity of
Berkeley High & elsewhere

autos swishing & switching
in it by the minute
as again it
does its thing
to me a nobody
bopping down streets
with my girlfriend
our raggedy bicycle
sack of Sunday grocery

fresh out the U-Save
as sun disguised
as moon like eyes
focus in on us —

Evolved ants, like
we don't take no chance
— our eyes look down
for heavens.

                                                    1965

ABSENT FROM THE UNITED STATES
(*Ausente de los Estados Unidos*)

for Edith, Tissa, Roger & Glen

O there's a laughy light
off our moon tonite

Theyre up driving around in their big Impalas
I'm down here by the Lake in Chapala

turning out murals

checking out burros!

                                        Mexico, 1965

MADNESS

Five thousand lovers I would have taken
& liters of rum upended,
the kilos of marijuana,
pills washed down,
grain upon grain of sand injected
— all for 5 pure minutes of happiness,
the pursuit of

nowhere. Yes & for paradise,
darlings, for realms I've yet to enter,
I would have ended up indulging this self
endlessly

1965

DOCK SONG CRAZY

Wharf of singleness
Wharf of water
send the winds
to mate my daughter
mate my daughter
deepen my son
run up hoists
when it's all done

Wharf of singleness
Wharf of water
Wharf the fog
in ablest weather
ablest weather

sweet as feathers
tackle my locker
& ship me ahoy

1966

ARABIA

Arabia it's so fine so hot
all that sand
up your nose
in your hair
the sun means torpor
at night means to freeze
(I am describing the desert of course)

I have never been to Arabia
I have met many Arabs
I once played drums in an Arab band
traveled with Arabs thru the Upper Peninsula
        (Michigan)

The first straight-out Arab I ever met
        was Fred Salah in junior high
        who was a big joker &
        had lots of brothers,
then when I was a busboy I knew an Egyptian
        who'd be hurrying to get home
        & catch Radio Cairo on the shortwave:
        "The only real news," he'd say,
Ive met lots of others altho
the majority Ive never laid eyes upon

I was inspired to take up Islam at 15,
the faith is inspiring leading as it does

to the beauty of all faiths pointing
as they do the way to God the One
                    God the Only,
I took for myself the name Ali
        — name of a cousin to the Prophet,
                    his first convert,
I no longer read the Qur'an
but shall seek always the Peace
        it
            is
                promising

I may have been an Arab myself,
no blue-eyed character for the motion pictures
                    but
Arabian like the given horse of proverbs
        into whose mouth you have not looked

                                    1966

DEAR RAVI SHANKAR

I have not entered the raga
I have only stood in the doorway
    to be pulled in
                & taken over

I once went to hear you
in a large room
full of (I hate to say it)
    full of stygian silence
but you cut thru the gloom

emerging slowly
　　out of the incensed walls
　　　　of our natural yearning
　　　　　　for heaven

　　　　　　　　　　　　　　　1966

IT'S INDIA

This magic land of sun stars
— all the hunger & dung
　　of mortal existence
　　that once set me
　　destroying myself
　　in youthful heroism

I bow to you for sending us
in the form of eternal loans
　　your brightest stars
　　Yogis
that dazzling sun of all Suns
　　Vedanta,
　　O beautiful rishi Vedas,
clarity I craved all my darkness
sought madly in my madness
　　our ignorance
　　the fathomlessness of which
　　is well preserved

I now know that you have suffered
for reasons out of your past
　　(my own included)
　　but
　　re-rising
　　you send us

lotuses
& to you for us
please accept
these inkling seeds of Thank You

1966

SUICIDE

Weekly I am murdering
& getting myself
murdered in Vietnam & elsewhere
roasted by napalm,
ambushed & bombed.

I am my teenage father
the ground soldier,
semen intact,
blown up out of proportion,
exploded systematically,
as tho some device
were properly programmed
to yank every boy-child
from his school path
in order to set fire
to the cereal-nourished flesh
in a flash — as from the light
of TV screens in rooms at night
shifting from sleep scene to holocaust.

Maggots at my dead mind,
I shuffle back among the mothers
who are modest of breast,
their very eyes beautiful,
as they arrive from schoolrooms

& who later provide me with wombs
to hide back up inside.

All afternoon next to dirt
I am digging the Top Ten
& dreaming backhome the comforts,
refreshed by six-paks, dozing off
front of "The Late Show," mmm Rice-A-Roni,
bunnies.
                My girlfriend writes, "Dear Love,
Dad just bought Mom a new Caliente
& today we all raced (me in my sweet Sprite)
up & down the new Freeway."

                    ▼   ▼   ▼

Who am I but the little mother who waits & waits,
pubescent father who keeps getting it, a
groovy little soldierboy gorged on
World War Two re-runs?
                I am the bilious
Powers-That-Be giving the orders
& those kept busy filling them.
                    Am I not
the girl left behind or even the boy Dad Mom
new car bomb napalm beer & other fine products
the food the tube hit tunes blasting
down the Freeway to freedom?

                                        1966

PALM DRIVE PALO ALTO

We move already thru a low-pitched heaven
flesh blending into eucalyptus
trees becoming air producing
clouds on into sky into ether
out to inner space,
leaving nothing out,
leaving all there is

1966

KICKING

for Sergio Mondragón

Nothing to it, man.
A new star comes up
only this time from inside you
& you do the frantic dance
you been doing all along
only now youre all alone

▾   ▾   ▾

God is peeping at you
right out your own eye
& from all the eyes of space

God is even in the edge of a cigarette
beheld from great distances.
A leg of roast lamb
stretched out with martini
is God taken hungrily, elastically
& without meditation

[311]

▼   ▼   ▼

"Spiritual combat
is as brutal
as the battle of men." (Rimbaud)
& also there is gentle Kay Johnson
with her "clumps of God everywhere"
to fall back on
when there's agony, lulls

▼   ▼   ▼

I prefer the not thinking of it,
letting these eyes tastes & cells of mind
scrape up against one another
to establish that hole
finally thru which I tumble
clean, thru

▼   ▼   ▼

Old foul habits,
painful practices,
kicked the same way
we keep kicking pasts

in the mind

in time

1967

SEVENTH APRIL

How beautiful you are
given to me
to appreciate

I take excursions
up into my lonely self
& wait for you
rather than float out
to miss you
waiting

These sadnesses,
drynesses of our times
will give way
to light-new splendor

& finding you
I'll have returned
to my very self,
the dream solved,
mysteries shaken,
all absence removed,
each touch intact

How beautiful

1967

NOW'S THE TIME

for Gordon Lapides

7:47 a.m.
Charles Parker's message from 1946
or whenever it was teaches us

that beautiful eternities dwell inside moments
& reverberating forever
charge us with godliness of creation,
creating by the moment,
ignorance of which
brings us to dead end
upon dead end. I am not anything less
than soul shedding layer after layer
of no-soul that soul may reveal itself
to itself so to speak,
an unvicious actually joyous
circle of commitment & revelation ensues

but you got to get in that groove,
you got to take chances &
avoid romances of daydream
which is no-dream really
but imprisonment,
the door closing,
tears crop up
in automatic
misery
vs.
freedom,

atoms becoming atoms
the earth is built
to crumble away
as God smiles
crumbling begins, ends,
the smiling goes on,

you happen,
keep happening.

Place: everywhere
Time: Now —

7:54 a.m.

1967

DREAMJOT: 1962

He stood before her
in a dark color foldout of Mexico,
his body surrounding him
& all his blues dissolving in the yellow air.
She was the approacher
who said things,
fur under her meat arms
warm
on the rooftop where they met.
She spread her whole nervous system
down by his side
fluttering,
dewy to the roots of her hair.
The marimba band below bopped on
to the thonk of pesos & centavos.
She spread her lips to say nothing.
He understood & went crazy
sniffing her everywhere:
in the tule trees, rainwater, buses, ruins, dust.
She smiled her teeth
& again they were in the diner
off the zócalo
run by the Japanese wed to the Indian girl

in another dream
from another life
for the first time
noticing one another.
he wanted to inhabit her forever
but
dying
didnt,
his stupid heart
atop Mt. Popo
pounding

1967

SOME SPICE FOR JACK SPICER

Well anyway even tho
it isnt likely I'll be asking any poem out
to the pictures tonight for a giggle
or for a thrilling motorcycle ride
or up to some loft with a band
for a couple of beers
or a toke or two
& kisses
on some midsummer balcony
in starry Veracruz by the sea
it's still too beautiful
for words or touch
this business of existence
when you can sit back away from it,
I know.
You know it too.
We all know it
but poems show it.
Aside from being

"almost blind like a camera"
poetry *is*,
is — that's all!
But now you take a poet —
I mean, *you* take a poet!
I'll take ineffable bliss
everytime:
the knowing
(when I'm safe in my true mind)
that poetry
like energy
or whatever the latest explanation
for the basis of our being here together
knows no barrier
no slow motion & no speed up
only electrification & sorriness
& even a lemon
can get mangled in translation
from everywhere to some place.
Peacefully I shake your hand
& bid you rest well in spiritland
where love
as here
must be purer than music
carried on the wind
& infinitely less assailable

1968

THE MYTH SCIENCE OF OUR TIME

Sun Ra
  Roi
    Ho
      Che
        Mao
          Giap
            Rap
              Fidel
                Babu
                  Trane

1968

DANCING NAKED

I honor you,
I point to Genesis in the Bible
& affirm that I'm as much Adam
as you are Eve.
Our inner worlds
not only eclipse one another
but shine as proof
that text is text
& sex is sex.

Love
on the other hand
has endless angles.
To say that God loves us
is still to me
the whole beautiful point
more factual than any other truth.
To say that I love you

can be merely a gesture
or in grander instances
a pocket-sized version
of the real thing.

Just as sure as the green berries
sprouting along the limbs
of this unidentified plant
are already turning a surprise red
in the fresh air & sunshine
of our kitchen window,
my knowledge & love of you
is something that grows & grows
even as we flower
between cracks in
the mad cement walkways of our time
avoiding in slow motion
what a molotov cocktail does;
even as we flower in room after room
together
or alone by the Pacific
sailing
nonstop
thru life
with all its suffering
& delicious stretches
on into contemporary heaven
maybe in time for the honorable mentions

1968

THE LEADBELLY SONG

Yes I'm glad
blood signature or no
& that walking
you talk about
I done all that
walked all the way
from Detroit
to California
& didnt stop once
to pluck the thorns
out of my brain,
met some pretty gals,
kissed to the song
went to war
a photograph of me
on one side
& on the other
in the distance
snorting like a stuck bull
myself in flames
stomping forward
to tangle ass
a bomb went off
cherry smelling,
got guitars thrown at me
& I was spared
the chain gang

ah, but you could sing
cities & ashes
& brown/black/meat
wobbling thru your songs
bullets flying
western cowboys
the space between
train tracks
widening before us

green grass
corn
heaven
pictures & energy
pouring from you
like rainwater
trickling down a branch
I caught the fever
called off the war
put everything away
stopped walking
stopped talking
moved in with Jean Harlow
bought that horse
Stewball
on a Monday
& kissed Irene
goodnight

flopped over
grew my hair out
picked up on your jive
fingers tingling
wrapped around
a new hammer

1968

JACKIE McLEAN: ALTO SAXOPHONE

I
am
forced
to realize
that written

he (the horn player)
gets that unmistakably successful
Iron Age sound:
ripe screams
down elevator shafts
in buildings the upper storeys of which
no artist would prize as loft

I say he's a sun-bound Bird
descendant
: the prestidigitator
sure enough
producer of metal flowers
for that's what grows simplest
twixt cracks
in the skin
of a concrete world
of alloyed beams

Ah but flaming within is God's pure orchid
whispering its hearty language
in heady fragrances

Listen
&
glisten
in the aggravation-produced joy
uniting jazz children
the world over

1965–1968
Berkeley, Mexico D.F., Detroit, Palo Alto

STILL LIVES

One of those impossibly lonely
nights, deliciously lonely —
no star, no heat, no street;
only a table by a window
a beer a cup of tea
God thundering in your blood.
You feel how the Temptations
are right: it *does* go deeper
than the eye can view.
Even the world with soot
& light covering it will appear as mystery
with room enough for love:
jealousy's follow-up;
a room where sex
has to humble itself.

1969

THE ODDS

Who knows where you go
even while I'm sitting
at the table across from you
or lying drowsy in bed
pillow to pillow, blanketed
like a woolen sky
pulled up around our heads?
When I dream the sky
is yellow or water & sun-
light with angels gliding
thru layers of laughter
where the tree we sat under
was only a quiet male loquat

bearing no fruit but leaves.
I leave you mornings
in the industrial age guessing
not only if I'll ever come back
but what the chances are
I'll be approximately the same.
It almost never works;
I'm almost never the same,
but neither are you.
Life becomes a sullen game
of give & take in which
the giver takes all, or
taker gives all.
There are no losers.

1969

OCTOBER WINDOW

Today clouds come to visit
the lemontree the plumtrees
the balding figtree backdoor
with persimmons fit to burst
outside around a fatter window
right angles away from this
lonely modern aluminum window
designed not to open or shut

Back in my old falltime Michigans
with Ohios & Indianas pulling
at the edges this sunless day
is still a staple & reason enough
for getting down to business
with the business of facts

Darkening before me now at
midday telephone poles &
tall & taller evergreens strung with
obnoxious cable that gets in
the way of dreaming (space being
my only access to a sealed-off
crop of sky) this October window
lights things up here indoors

Once the rain starts to fall
I'll feel free & happy all over again

                                        Veterans Day, 1972

LOOK GOOD, SMELL GOOD, FEEL

Something like the way
this sentry plant
stands so simply there

It doesn't hiccup,
it doesn't go bananas,
it stands & just grows

thru centuries, no?
thru rain & drought
as matters of course

Maybe like bamboo
it's really trying to
tell us something

Can you tune in its
ecstatic frequency?
Please, what is it saying?

1972

FOR JANET KAFKA, DEAD AT 30

It was as though we met at McDonald's
on Christmas Day, our cars melting the snow
outside while we dashed in to order Ronald's
Big Mac, french fries, Cokes and ketchup to go.

1976

DEXTER GORDON AT KEYSTONE KORNER

A bebopper in his soul, he sends
you back down paths you haven't
scampered since the day you first
discovered music could not only talk to you
but that you could talk back to it
as well, inside out yet

1977

A POEM FOR DOROTHY DANDRIDGE

Sweet Dorothy, I know you're still
out there somewhere, swallowing
with flashing eyes — everybody's
closet gypsy fantasy, still a gas,
a ghost, eternally awash in seas and
high up among the closely watched.

Dear Star, when I look up to take in
All those mounds of mocha and good hair,
I can't help but ask my heart: Well,
if she can't make it then nobody can,
certainly no lovely American spook;
not even with good acting thrown in to boot.

There was this movie on TV late
the other night where you and some lover
were going through hell across
some dramatic hospital bed, yet in your head
(I think I could tell) you were listening
to some other bell chiming time, chiming you.

The world will never know much of anything
about you, and neither will I, but
there's an itch I get watching this charade
to ask your mama, the great actress maid,
about these sapphires, all these pearls
        and rubies bright as stars.

1982

POLITICS AS HISTORY

Mechanics have always been the same;
it's press focus and pressure that varies.
We know that George Washington, like
Ulysses S. Grant, Woodrow Wilson and
either Roosevelt, had their Waterloos
and Watergates too, but that they didn't
have to live in the public armpit. Well,
the game is still the same and it goes
on and on like this: Find yourself an
untapped trapdoor into history and use it.

1980

WINTER LEAVES

Sometimes you love someone
so much you have to leave them
alone with their memories of
how love's become whatever
it is & leave it at that, leave
it left in order to leaf it &
flutter in the wind the way leaves
leave trees & like trees leave
leaves; mute like light in a
rakish, unsorted sort of way.

Sometimes you retrace the cycles
of love &, surprised by fingertip
discoveries, you touch upon cycles
of love as incalculable as the inner
targets of tree trunks whose circles
are true & enfold the very way a rose
unpeels petal by petal into bullseye
essence: a remembered space that

can't be so much measured as sniffed
in November, December, January when
tides, prices & expectations are on
the rise; nothing but frosty departure.

Hardly measurable, barely touched,
sometimes you love someone
so much you have to leave them loved.

1980

TUNE

Say we were pushed to name a time
    when rhythm didn't exist —
that would be like trying to box
    without making a fist.

Like footprints, there is no one beat
    that change will not erase;
the earth ticks on yet holds its mold
    in patterns that light space.

The love of being regular
    is old as tides or sands
or being female once a month;
    breath, heart thumps, drums or hands.

This time to which we dance our lives
    is real down to our smiles,
our dyings, our talk, our years; the leaps
    from stages into aisles.

1980

THE AFTERNOON AFTER

Drowsy with beauty, I bathe &
haunt this slow-falling afternoon
needled with rain where
my dream-weary eye stops
at a portion of window suddenly
beginning to warm with late
sunlight. What is the tipsy
urgency pushing me to sully this
page with language from an island,
a very shrinking I-Land encircled
at this hour by violet light?

Now doused with motion & notions of
a sea-change, the wayward ghost
of me is on some ocean now, leaving
space between us so unattended that
I can't quite keep up with it all:
the shifts, the cooling light,
the memory of summer in this room;
scratches from a green, bracing hike
in the winding, forested foothills
of this town where abandon, like
the warmth of colored voices at last
night's winning dinner party,
was heavy with pleasure for a change.

And dozing with the pregnant air,
this light that I can feel
flickering all up & down Ash Street
this fallen afternoon, I look out &
finally surrender to a calming voice
within that says, "Even poetry,
like taking a bath, has its limits;
the bottom line." The lyric line too
invisibly begins & seems to end
where afternoon & midnight blend.

1981

HOT HOUSE

Embryonic or symphonic
the sun on glass effect
of this rhythm is torrid

Florid in their nearness
fragrant light reigns
& slow time breathes

Even the orchid has
catches: an orchestra
hides in her color, her O

Sweet conjugal love is
not beyond this sound
where New York meets Puri

In the softest blur
of time & its rivers
the heat of dreams arrives

1989

LEAVING ROCHESTER

In perfect printed breath
old desire patterns
mist up the windows
of this morning's Trailways
Bus bound for sleepy Syracuse

And what desire powers me
now that the storm is on,
now that wet & snowy fog is

racing straight ahead, all
tree-lined in the heatless light?

Once the spiritualist hub
of the New World, Rochester keeps
updating her "St. Lawrence Blues"
with flour, apples, cherries, music;
this is Xerox & Kodak's Xanadu.

Around this racing, bumptious bus
there is no village that encapsulates
the soul like flesh & thought.
Breath, let all my morning wanting
exhale itself into the perfect
emptiness of afternoon.

Let noon soon lose
its moodiness in Syracuse,
infused with nightlessness.

1989

LEAVING SYRACUSE

All these girls licking & sucking
their own twitchy fingers free of chocolate
were winos once on well-policed benches,
or smoking in urine-lined johns.

The lyrical light of Greyhound,
its bright snowiness the color of Rip
Van Winkle's beard, erect with winter,
lushes up the loveliest of valleys.
Those trucks & barns & frozen

slopes as up-and-down as chimney smoke
give you plenty to shine on.

Joy is with us all the time
we're being bused from one universe
to the next. Dappled or evenly iced over,
these subtle imitations of life keep
on the move. Good morning, Rochester,
have you heard the news?

1989

WATSONVILLE AFTER THE QUAKE

On Central Coast radio KTOM blasts
Eddie Rabbitt thru waves of air the sea
surrounds, & all the other country stars
come out (Claude King, Tammy Wynette, Shelley
West) & spread themselves in droplets.
The sacred moisture of their song is skin
to seal a pain that quavers in this ash-blue night
coming on just now like a downcast motel date,
who's warned you from in front that she'll be coming
'round the mountain when she comes.

Whose tents are these? What's with these shot
parking lot & alleyway families peeping around
the raggedy backs of undemolished fronts?
That brownskin kid on a grassy patch along Main,
catching a football & falling with joy
on the run, is his family up from Mazatlán,
up from Baja or Celaya — or edges of eternity?

Network TV didn't do this news up right.
For all their huff & puff & blow-your-house-down,

the mediators of disaster and distress
didn't find this sickly devastation sexy.
Besides, who's going to cry or lose sleep
over a spaced-out, tar-papered, toppled-down town
by the sea, brown now with alien debris?

1989

A POEM FOR DYLAN THOMAS

When night moved through the air
of that almighty sleep, you stumbled.

I dove fast to catch you falling there,
undreamed, the drowsing king of consonance.
And in that mirrored state, the whole
of Wales ignored, you dragged me down at once
into your deep, bright, ringing countryside.

There are no names for lines as yet unsung,
that hang, that dangle scantly from
the heart's tight, high-wired rope.
Hope is what your songs stirred up in me.
They left me with no choice; I went right on
voicing all I'd heard and seen and breathed
down there inside your dream, and mixed it well
with wishes and bewitchments of my own.

We probed all nights together separately.
And daylight was never so gentle as it was
the medicinal afternoon you woke and slipped away
to smell the sweet, brisk air; to swallow
the sea — all small-craft warnings be damned.

1990

POEM INDEX

FIRST LINE INDEX

Evening isnt so much a
    playland as it is, 84

Far away, I suppose you could
    say, 181
Fifteen years up & her tongue's
    still flapping, 116
Finally you sit, 170
First light of day in Mississippi,
    52
Five thousand lovers I would
    have taken, 305
Floating thru morning, 59
Fly on into my poem, 22
For the aging hipster, 43
From looking at things Navajo,
    218
From the soothing distance,
    256

Get that feeling sometimes, 76
Glorious, nourishing,
    flourishing moon, swollen
    with, 253
Going back to D.F., 144
Good morning!, 111
Green is the color of
    everything, 85

Hands and arms and legs and
    mouths, 284
Hanging from fresh trees, 46
He mounts the stand &, 221
He ran his hands thru her hair,
    148
He stood before her, 315
Heartbreak October moon of
    sun, 243
Here, 45
Here in violet light, 237
His whole world revolves
    around light dark, 168
How beautiful you are, 313

How much of me is sandwiches
    radio beer?, 86
How overwhelming, 87
How quickly morphology, 65
Human love is all electrical, a
    whirring, 261
Humming like a hawk in
    motion, 190

I, 321
I can't keep up with your love
    anymore, 222
I couldnt ever tell you, 47
I don't ask to be forgiven, 194
I draw hats on rabbits, sew
    women back, 78
I first saw you in a trance, 60
I have not entered the raga,
    307
I honor you, 318
I leave you on that downtown
    street of, 128
I love the quiet, hard, 227
I love you, 35
I owe you this picture:, 207
I see it zooming down, 138
I thirst for, 158
I too, 64
I violinize peace, 72
I'm going to be just like you,
    Ma, 18
I'm just happy to be being, 303
If this is showbiz, then am I,
    277
If you can't finance it
    undercover, 269
In 15 minutes, 145
In a tobacco trance, 272
In a twinkling, the green, 240
In audible dreams I'm forever
    going back, 183
In glassy, incandescent glory,
    278

Books

Dancing (poems), Corinth Books, New York, 1969.

Snakes (novel), Holt, Rinehart & Winston, New York 1970, Sidgwick & Jackson, London, 1971; Dell Laurel Edition, 1972; Creative Arts Book Co., Berkeley, 1980.

The Song Turning Back into Itself (poems), Holt, Rinehart & Winston, New York, 1971.

Who Is Angelina? (novel), Holt, Rinehart & Winston, New York, 1975; Sidgwick & Jackson, London, 1978; *Chi È Angelina?* (Italian translation by Luciano Federighi), Jacabook, Milano, 1983.

Geography of the Near Past (poems), Holt, Rinehart & Winston, New York, 1976.

Sitting Pretty (novel), Holt, Rinehart &Winston, New York, 1976; New American Library, New York, 1977; Parla Sitting Pretty (Italian translation by Luciano Federighi), Jacabook, Milano, 1985; Creative Arts Book Co. (10th Anniversary edition), Berkeley, 1986.

Ask Me Now (novel), McGraw Hill, New York, 1980; Sidgwick & Jackson, London, 1980.

Bodies & Soul (musical memoirs), Creative Arts Book Co., Berkeley, 1981.

The Blues Don't Change: New and Selected Poems, Louisiana State University Press, Baton Rouge, 1982.

Kinds of Blue (musical memoirs), Creative Arts Book Co., Berkeley, 1984.

Things Ain't What They Used to Be (musical memoirs), Creative Arts Book Co., Berkeley, 1987.

Seduction by Light (novel), Delacorte/Seymour Lawrence, New York, 1988.

Mingus/Mingus: Two Memiors (with Janet Coleman), Creative Arts Book Co., Fall 1989

Heaven: Poems 1956-1990, Creative Arts Book Co. 1992.

Co-Editor

Calafía: The California Poetry (with Ishmael Reed, et al), a
Y'Bird Book, Berkeley, 1979.

Yardbird Lives! (with Ishmael Reed), Grove Press, New York,
1978.

Screenplays

Nigger (feature-length motion picture based on Dick Gregory's
autobiography; for director-producer Joseph Strick's Laser
Fils, Inc. New York, 1972.

Sparkle (dramatic treatment for feature-length film); for the
Robert Stigwood Organization, New York and London, 1972.

A Piece of the Action (participating writer for feature-length film
starring Bill Cosby and Sidney Poitier); for Verdon
Productions, Hollywood, 1975.

Sitting Pretty (an as yet unfilmed feature-length motion picture
based on the novel by Al Young); for First Artists
Productions Ltd, Burbank, 1977.

Bustin' Loose (participating writer for feature-length film
starring Richard Pryor and Cicely Tyson); for Universal
Pictures, Universal City, 1979.

Personal Problems (co-writer with Ishmael Reed of this 2-hour
pilot for a TV soap opera); for Robert Polidor Productions,
New York, 1982.

The Stars and their Courses (co-writer with William Rose of this
award-winning, 45-minute dramatic film); for William Rose
Productions; Palo Alto, CA, 1983.

Al Young   Bhopal, India

Al Young

Born May 31, 1939, at Ocean Springs, Mississippi, Al Young
spent his first decade in the coastal and rural South and his
second in and near Detroit, Michigan. By the age of three he
had learned to read and, while still in his teens, he published
poems, stories and articles in local newspapers, periodicals and
small press publications. From 1957–61 he attended the
University of Michigan at Ann Arbor, where he majored in
Spanish with the goal of becoming a language teacher who
wrote novels and books of poetry on the side. He did not
complete his Bachelors of Arts degree until 1969, when he
graduated with honors from the University of California at
Berkeley. During the intervening years, Young continued to
write and publish his work in literary journals while working
at a variety of jobs. He has been a professional musician (a
guitarist and singer), a disk jockey, medical photographer,
warehouseman, clerk-typist, yard clerk for the Southern Pacific
Railroad, interviewer for the California Department of
Employment, lab aide and industrial films narrator. He has
never taught Spanish, but his travels include Spain, Mexico,
Portugal, France, England, Yugoslavia, Hong Kong, Singapore,
Australia, India, Canada and the whole of the United States,
where he has lectured and read from his work extensively.
Widely anthologized, Young's poetry, fiction and essays have
been translated into more than a dozen languages, including
German, Norwegian, Swedish, Serbo-Croatian, Italian,
Japanese, Chinese and Spanish. *Harper's*, *The New York Times*,
Rolling Stone, *Essence*, *Paris Review*, *Ploughshares*, *The Chicago
Sun-Times*, *Iowa Review*, *Callaloo* and *New Directions* are some
of the places where his work has appeared. As a screenwriter,
Al Young has written scripts for Sidney Poitier, Bill Cosby and
Richard Pryor. With poet-novelist Ishmael Reed, he was a
founding editor of the legendary *Yardbird Reader*, the multi-
cultural arts journal whose pioneering spirit lives on in their
magazine, *Quilt*. The recipient of numerous honors and awards
(which include NEA, Fulbright and Guggenheim fellowships),
Mr. Young has been Lecturer in Literature and Creative Writing
at the University of California at Santa Cruz and is Visiting
Professor of English at the University of Michigan. For most
of his life, he has lived in the San Francisco Bay Area.